THE ROYAL BRITISH LEGION

GOLDEN
BOOK OF
REMEMBRANCE

A TRIBUTE TO THOSE WHO SERVED

HENRY BUCKTON

ASHFORD, BUCHAN & ENRIGHT
LEATHERHEAD

Golden Book of Remembrance

First published in 1995 by
Ashford Buchan & Enright, publishers
P.O. Box 20, Leatherhead, Surrey KT24 5HH

British Library Cataloguing in Publication Data

ISBN 1 85253 311 0

Layout and typesetting by Priory Publications, Haywards Heath

Printed in England by
FotoDirect Ltd., Brighton

CONTENTS

2nd Lieutenant Henry Buckton (the author) and, right, with his children Emily and Jason, while an AUO with the Light Infantry Cadet Battalion.

The author marches at the head of the uniformed organizations on their way to the Glastonbury Cenotaph, on Remembrance Sunday 1994.
(Photos: Henry Buckton)

FOREWORD

Poppies, the mud of Flanders fields, the blood of those that died in the war to end wars. And then, twenty-one years later, a second world war.

Poppies, the colour of blood, to remind us.

The freedom that we enjoy – freedom to speak our minds, to protest, to lobby our leaders, to lampoon them, to shout from the rooftops – all the freedoms we take for granted are not ours of right. They have been fought for. They will always have to be fought for.

Never must we take freedom for granted.

That is what this 'Golden Book of Remembrance' is about. There are quotes here from all sorts of men and women, words dredged from their inner being to express their feelings and their need in moments of desperation, words fashioned out of the agony of war.

Lest we forget:– These words, falling off the tongue, often so glibly now that the menace of occupation is no longer with us and the names on the memorials are, most of them, no longer people remembered, but simply names . . . . LEST WE FORGET: those three words should for ever remain etched on our hearts.

Fifty years have now gone by since the death camp gates were forced open to reveal the horrors within, fifty years since Europe was finally liberated. In the pages that follow the men and women who stood alone when the world was dark and all hope gone, give voice to their feelings. Some of them are dead now, but their words live on to evoke the extraordinary mood that gripped us as the bombs fell and the Battle of Britain was fought over our heads.

It was a mood that persisted through the long years of war, but never with quite the same intensity. Shakespeare said it all in that great speech, which might well have been Churchill broadcasting to the nation . . . .

Hammond Innes

5

The Queen's Speech
at The Guildhall, Portsmouth,
on Saturday, 4th June, 1994

Operation Overlord was the product of meticulous planning, secrecy amazingly preserved, and the closest possible cooperation between Britain and her Allies, especially those from across the Atlantic. The scale of the operation was unprecedented – nearly two hundred thousand men, some five thousand ships and eleven thousand aircraft were involved. To gain great victories, great risks must be taken and so they were on D-Day, in spite of the strength of the Allied forces. But calculated boldness was blessed by good fortune, and rewarded eventually by success.

All the planning and the force of arms would, however, have fallen short had it not been for the heroism of those who took part. They were, predominantly, young men – some of them very young. Most of them had foregone, through the years of war, their carefree youth. They had, instead, borne the awesome responsibility of fighting for their country, for a free world and for a lasting peace. As they gathered here in Portsmouth and all over the South of England in the months leading up to June 1944, I wonder if they realised just how high were the stakes, and how those of us at home were watching and praying for them as they prepared for a campaign which would lead to the liberation of the whole of occupied Europe.

Over the next few days, we shall recall, in different places and in different ways, their courage and their sacrifice. Many veterans will be in Normandy themselves, retracing their steps up the beaches and beyond, amidst altered landmarks. Others will prefer to remember quietly their comrades who fell that day. For, lest we forget, there were some ten thousand casualties on D-Day itself. In the aftermath, the figure rose until, by the Autumn, some thirty seven thousand of the Allied Forces had been killed, among them many gallant French citizens.

A great debt is owed to those who made that sacrifice, to all those who fought in the Normandy campaign, and, not least, to the men and women of the auxiliary organisations who, in diverse ways and with selfless dedication, made the operation possible.

On 6th June 1944, my father spoke to this Nation and to the Empire, urging his peoples to pray for the success of that huge enterprise. "Four years ago", he said, "our Nation and Empire stood alone against an overwhelming enemy, with our backs to the wall. Tested as never before in our history, in God's providence we survived the test; the spirit of the people, resolute, dedicated, burned like a bright flame, lit surely from those Unseen Fires which nothing can quench.

Now once more a supreme test has to be faced. This time the challenge is not to fight to survive but to fight to win the final victory for the good cause. We and our Allies are sure that our fight is against evil and for a world in which goodness and honour may be the foundation of the life of men in every land."

As we know, those prayers were answered with victory, earned in Normandy and in other theatres of war by all those who fought in the Allied cause. But since then, we have seen that the peace which victory brought is a fragile thing. Events round the world, some of them close to home in Europe, prove that to us day after day. It is up to us to make sure that the prayers of fifty years ago are truly answered, by re-dedicating ourselves to the creation of a world at peace.

Operation Overlord was a mighty deed, which proved what can be achieved, against daunting odds, when Governments and peoples act together with conviction in a common cause. We are right to look back on it with pride, and with thanks to God for its success. But we cannot let it rest there.

We must keep faith with those who landed on the beaches of Normandy fifty years ago, by continuing vigilant in defence of peace and freedom. This commemoration has brought the past into the present: may it also be an inspiration for the future.

(Reproduced with the kind permission of Her Majesty The Queen (Patron of the Royal British Legion). With special thanks to Sir Kenneth Scott, Private Secretary to the Queen, for preparing Her speeches for publication.)

BUCKINGHAM PALACE

THE QUEEN'S SPEECH AT ARROMANCHES ON MONDAY, 6TH JUNE,1994

Monsieur le Maire, thank you for the welcome which you and the citizens of Arromanches have extended to Prince Philip, to me and to all our countrymen. I am glad that the Government of France is represented here by Madame Simone Veil. By the courage which she and a multitude like her displayed in the Nazi concentration camps, she represents perfectly why we are here today - to remember and to give thanks for deliverance.

This town and this beach must hold a unique place in the memories of those of you who were here in June 1944. I am proud to see so many veterans of Operation Overlord, one of the most remarkable amphibious operations ever accomplished. You, and the widows of those who fought, will be remembering the deeds that were done that day, the comrades and husbands who never returned, and those who did come home but sadly are no longer with us.

D-Day was indeed the beginning of the end. The months of planning at home, of preparation by the French Resistance, all conducted in the utmost secrecy, culminated here in Normandy that day, beginning the Liberation first of France and finally of Europe.

Many of you will have in your minds vivid pictures - some perhaps all too vivid - of that epic day, and of the heroism and endurance shown by our own troops and by our Allies. Those of us who were far away can only imagine what it was like, and stand back in admiration of those who planned and fought for the establishment of that hard-won bridgehead.

It was you, and your comrades and Allies fighting on other fronts, who delivered Europe from that yoke of organised barbarism from which the men and women of following generations have been mercifully free. They should remember that they owe that freedom to those who fought and defeated Nazism. Next year we shall commemorate the fiftieth anniversary of the end of the Second World War. Old adversaries are now reconciled. But the Europe which we know today could not exist had not the tide of war been turned here in Normandy fifty years ago.

Veterans of the Normandy campaign, you deserve your nation's thanks. May we, your fellow countrymen, be worthy of what you did for us.

The Queen's Speech at Arromanches on Monday, 6th June 1994

Monsieur le Maire, thank you for the welcome which you and the citizens of Arromanches have extended to Prince Philip, to me and to all our countrymen. I am glad that the Government of France is represented here by Madame Simone Veil. By the courage which she and a multitude like her displayed in the Nazi concentration camps, she represents perfectly why we are here today – to remember and to give thanks for deliverance.

This town and this beach must hold a unique place in the memories of those of you who were here in June 1944. I am proud to see so many veterans of Operation Overlord, one of the most remarkable amphibious operations ever accomplished. You, and the widows of those who fought, will be remembering the deeds that were done that day, the comrades and husbands who never returned, and those who did come home but sadly are no longer with us.

D-Day was indeed the beginning of the end. The months of planning at home, of preparation by the French Resistance, all conducted in the utmost secrecy, culminated here in Normandy that day, beginning the Liberation first of France and finally of Europe.

Many of you will have in your minds vivid pictures – some perhaps all too vivid – of that epic day, and of the heroism and endurance shown by our own troops and by our Allies. Those of us who were far away can only imagine what it was like, and stand back in admiration of those who planned and fought for the establishment of that hard-won bridgehead.

It was you, and your comrades and Allies fighting on other fronts, who delivered Europe from that yoke of organised barbarism from which the men and women of following generations have been mercifully free. They should remember that they owe that freedom to those who fought and defeated Nazism. Next year we shall commemorate the fiftieth anniversary of the end of the Second World War. Old adversaries are now reconciled. But the Europe which we know today could not exist had not the tide of war been turned here in Normandy fifty years ago.

Veterans of the Normandy campaign, you deserve your nation's thanks. May we, your fellow countrymen, be worthy of what you did for us.

(Reproduced with the kind permission of Her Majesty The Queen (Patron of the Royal British Legion). With special thanks to Sir Kenneth Scott, Private Secretary to the Queen, for preparing Her speeches for publication.)

Left: The War Memorial at East Brent in Somerset, designed by the author's great-grandfather, Mr George Derrick, and upon which a Derrick is listed among the Glorious Dead. (Photo: Henry Buckton)

Facing page: George Derrick is pictured here (centre row, second left) with soldiers of the South Wales Borderers at Burnham-on-Sea during the First World War. The author's grand-mother is the little girl held up in the back row. (Photo: Henry Buckton)

INTRODUCTION

As an Ordinary Member of St. James Central Branch of the Royal British Legion, I am very aware of the importance of keeping alive the great tradition of honouring and remembering those who have given their lives in the service of their country.

I have always been aware and interested in the subject of memorials, due to the fact that my great-grandfather, Mr George Derrick, who was a practising architect in Burnham-on-Sea, was the designer of the classic war memorial at East Brent in Somerset, on the A370 to Weston-super-Mare, and upon which a Derrick is listed among the Glorious Dead.

1995 marks the 50th Anniversary of the end of the Second World War. Every year on Remembrance Sunday we still pay homage to those who died. The aim of this book is to discuss and examine this tribute and its relevance to the future of our nation.

With the aid of many well known people who represent us either through government, the church, the armed forces, or the media, I hope that we have created a living memorial, which attempts to keep alive the spirit of remembrance at a time when our younger generations might so easily forget.

2nd Lieutenant Henry Buckton

10 DOWNING STREET
LONDON SWIA 2AA

THE PRIME MINISTER

I was born just two years before the end of the Second World War and thus remember nothing of it.

But the war is a vitally important part of the tapestry of our nation. As a result of it, the pattern of life in Britain changed dramatically and permanently. The peace, security and freedom which we have enjoyed since 1945 are ours because of the effort and sacrifice during the years of war of men and women across the country. They were ordinary people with ordinary dreams, looking forward with confidence as we do today. It is because their dreams were shattered that ours might be realised that we must never forget.

John Major

May 1994

CHAPTER ONE

THE LEGACY OF LIBERATION

Those who were born after the end of the Second World War have been able to grow up in a society which strongly reflects the freedoms for which an entire generation fought and often died. Memories from those times are an evergreen legacy, handed down from generation to generation. The stories we have heard our parents and grandparents tell and retell has given us a vivid impression of a special time in our nation's history that should never be forgotten.

Throughout this book you will read the words freedom and liberty time and time again.

John Major
The Prime Minister

I was born just two years before the end of the Second World War and thus remember nothing of it. But the war is a vitally important part of the tapestry of our nation. As a result of it, the pattern of life in Britain changed dramatically and permanently. The peace, security and freedom which we have enjoyed since 1945 are ours because of the effort and sacrifice during the years of war of men and women across the country. They were ordinary people with ordinary dreams, looking forward with confidence as we do today. It is because their dreams were shattered that ours might be realised that we must never forget.

Lord Wilson of Rievaulx KG OBE FRS

I hope that this 50th anniversary of the end of the Second World War will help us all to renew our faith with all those who gave their lives for us, and those who worked so hard for us during those dark, difficult days. I was born during the First World War, and my childhood memories from that time, are of my family's sorrows and joys, and later my own. It would be good to see the return of the one minute silence when we can remember not only 1918 but 1945 as well.

The sacrifices made must be remembered so that we may better value the freedoms we now enjoy and work continuously to avoid conflicts in the future.

Neil Kinnock MP

The men and women who sacrificed their youth and their lives in the Second World War were without question fighting for freedom. We who have inherited that freedom must keep it as our most precious asset by ensuring that the peace and justice won in 1945 are the condition of life for people throughout the World.

Ann Winterton MP

Many of my mother's brothers served in the Second World War (and one in the First) and survived. I feel grateful for the sacrifice of others to defend freedom against tyranny and I will always remember the men and women who gave so much at that time.

Frank Field MP

Those who fought, those who suffered, and those who died, that we may live in freedom, must never be forgotten, nor must the lessons of the 1930s be forgotten either.

So what exactly is meant by freedom and liberty? In the World of today we all too often overlook our freedoms and misunderstand their relevance. Some people even complain about their lack of freedom. Britain is far from being perfect but since the end of the war we have evolved into a society which cares for its pensioners, the education of its children, the health of its citizens, and the general welfare of the nation in its entirity. Some suggest that this has not always been the case.

Paul Flynn MP

As the first air raid sirens wailed in 1939 over Cardiff, my father lay on his deathbed. He was an 'under age' volunteer in the First World War. He was shot and imprisoned. He died embittered by his treatment from ungrateful Governments who had rewarded returning heroes with unemployment and poverty. In the 1930s his war pension was cut.

After the end of the Second World War, returning heroes were treated with far greater respect and appreciation of their achievements. This respect and appreciation has been maintained within the act of Remembrance now familiar to us all, once a year, on a special day set aside so that we might all contemplate the significance of their sacrifice.

Freedom can be looked at in the most basic of terms. In Britain we are free to follow whatever career we choose; free to marry which ever partner we desire; free to choose the amount of children we have; free to improve our standard of education and breadth of knowledge; free to choose our political representatives; free to follow our chosen faith; and of course, above all else, we have the freedom of speech and movement. Cynics among you may say to yourselves that none of these things are freedoms, they are your birth rights. Of course you'd be correct in thinking that, but all of these things are restricted in some part of the World. The simple act of leaving your home when you like is under restriction somewhere in the World. In some countries the goods you are free to purchase are merely the items dictated to you by the state. Television, cinema and literature are prime examples of freedom. All of these media and newspapers in particular are heavily censored and suppressed in major parts of the globe.

Tony Blair MP

I was born almost 10 years after the end of the Second World War, which my father had, of course, fought in. As I grew up and read about the war, it was not only the extraordinary bravery of the men and women of the

British forces that impressed me. It was also the knowledge that, but for their courage, my father would never have had the freedom to settle down and marry my mother. I would never have grown up in a country where people can say what they think, live the lives they choose, vote in and out their Government.

Time must never dim our memories of their fight for our freedom, their sacrifice for our gain. In these troubled times, more than ever, we must not forget. I will not forget and I will try to teach my young children, growing up nearly half a century later, not to forget either. Because when we forget the lessons of history, we repeat its mistakes.

Young people today are hungry for success and material gain. Everybody seems to want everything at breakneck speed. Status and standard of living seem to have got out of all proportion. No longer are we satisfied with keeping up with the Jones', we have to be ahead of them, pressured into thinking ourselves failures if we don't have as much, or more than our neighbours.

When this country went to war in 1939 things were very different. People didn't have, or expect to have the material wealth of the 90s. Yet an entire generation supported, almost without question, the cause of liberating the subjugated peoples of Europe. As individuals they had nothing to gain, certainly nothing financial or materialistic. They ventured forth on a wonderful crusade to liberate millions of oppressed human beings. And when most of Europe and much of Asia had fallen beneath the tyrannical and cruel regimes of occupation which oppressed the very liberty that our nation believed in, England fought on, virtually alone. It could have been very easy at that point to have ended hostilities. Adolf Hitler had no real desire to invade England who he maintained to be natural allies of Germany. He was quite ready to call a truce with England, as long as he was given a free hand in Europe. If England had accepted this uneasy peace, her citizens could have carried on with their lives oblivious to the holocaust and countless inhumanities that were being perpetrated. Instead, the nation chose to fight on alone. A fight which subjected our island fortress to 'The Battle of Britain' and the 'Blitz'. The people of

England proudly endured all that the Luftwaffe could throw at them, confident that one day good would prevail over evil and the World would once again be free.

Winston S. Churchill MP

Present and future generations, both in our own country and around the World, owe an unfathomable debt of gratitude to the 'Hero' generation of 1939/45 for standing firm against all the odds in the face of the Hitlerite aggression as epitomised by the gallantry of 'The Few' in the Battle of Britain. For six long years they endured, as men and women, military and civilians, the privations, horror and sacrifice of World War.

Thanks to one million British and Commonwealth soldiers who, together with an equal number of our gallant American allies, hurled themselves against Hitler's Atlantic Wall in the D-Day invasion, Europe was liberated and the World purged of the scourge of the Swastika.

As my Grandfather declared, once the War was over: "It was the British nation and race dwelling around the globe that had the Lionheart – I merely had the good fortune to be called upon to give the 'Roar'!" Those who fought, those who suffered and, above all, those who made the ultimate sacrifice that we who came after might live in freedom, shall never be forgotten. Their memory is immortal!

Lord (Yehudi) Menuhin

No country gave more of her heart and of her treasure or survived more by faith and vision than Great Britain during the Second World War. She stood alone with an uncompromising respect for those universal values beyond survival, for the only justification of a fighter's death is the quality of life he has defended.

This overriding sense of purpose was shared by every civilian who, for the first time in contemporary wars, shared the hazards of the battle field. From now on, as we have already seen in the Bosnian and Japanese cities and, on a lesser (because earlier) scale in Britain, it is the women and children who will be decimated as surely as the men.

Can 'remembrance' still conjure the quiet, stubborn resolve, which marked these heroic men and women, to build a harmony of convictions and values, an ambition which seems beyond the reach of the world's most powerful and populous states?

I speak not only from the heart but with the enduring memory of the spirit and courage of Great Britain at war, which I experienced at close quarters when I flew over three times to give concerts in camps, hospitals and factories. This image of man at his best will forever remain in my mind.

Sir Christopher Cockerell CBE FRS

Due to the German bombing, doodle-bugs and rockets, most of the country and the people living here were, unlike previous wars, in the front line. Our merchant seamen, for instance, were as much in the war as any of the Armed Forces. We had doodle-bugs overhead, one of them only about 100 feet up when its motor failed so that it came down. When living near Chelmsford, we also had a 500lb bomb land in a field just behind us, luckily in very soft ground so that most of the blast went upwards and all it did to us was to break some windows. When I went to look at the steep-sided crater about 20 feet deep, what interested me was that there were some large rounded boulders at the bottom of this soft ground, which had rolled down some 10,000 years ago under the last glacier. Essex was at the southern fringe of the glaciers.

Also, I had just called on de Havilland's, as our gear went in their aeroplanes, and I was going along outside the factory when there was a huge noise. I stopped the car, and there was a German bomber, so close that I could see the whites of the pilot's eyes, as he started to come up de Havilland's parallel to their runway, where all their air-raid shelters were, and his string of bombs killed about 350 people. He was a brave man, because he knew he would be brought down, and he was.

Sir Christopher Cockerell (photographed just before the outbreak of war) who worked on Marconi's 'Engines of War'. (See also page 55.)
(Photo: courtesy Sir Christopher Cockerell)

In many ways the act of Remembrance should therefore be a way of humbling the fast-paced, greedy and self-centred amongst us, into a realisation of the goodness there is in mankind. Although it is natural to want the best for ourselves and our families, we should also, ALL of us, be concerned with the rest of mankind and the world we live in. Remembrance is a lesson to each one of us, about ourselves and about the future of our planet.

Alan Beith MP

Some of those who have no direct experience of war feel themselves to be out of place at remembrance ceremonies, which they associate with those survivors and families who have vivid memories of comrades and loved ones who never returned. But why is it that so many of us have not been called upon to serve in war? Why is it that we all enjoy the freedom to say what we believe? Because so many were ready to give their lives to stop tyrants and to fight for our freedom. We must never forget that sacrifice, and, as other countries do, we must teach every new generation how much they owe to those who made it. As those who are left grow old, it falls to those who have derived the great benefits of peace and freedom in succeeding generations to say of the fallen, "We will remember them".

On Remembrance Sunday the nation as a whole pays homage to the millions of British and Commonwealth citizens who perished in the two World Wars. Although modern generations have little first hand experience of this kind of loss, most of us did infact have relatives killed in one or both of these conflicts. Remembrance Sunday can therefore be a personal experience to even the youngest.

Ian Bruce MP

Remembrance is important, not only as a tribute to those who have fallen, but as a continual reminder, particularly important for politicians, that we must do everything possible to preserve peace. Our acts of remembrance are most important to those of us who have not had to fight for our country and who do not have first-hand experience of loss.

My paternal grandfather, Joseph Bruce, died a few days after arriving at the front in Flanders, leaving a widow alone to bring up three small children. He knew nothing of his five grandchildren, nor the future that they inherited.

The constituency of South Dorset, which I represent in Parliament, has seen its sons and daughters die in wars around the world. Its war memorials bear stark testimony to how many fell and how many British and Allied troops left Dorset's shores for D-Day and the subsequent operations and whose last memory of Britain would have been our beautiful Dorset cliffs. As a marshalling area, everyone was involved on the home front and the Luftwaffe and the German E-boats regularly brought death to our shores. We shall remember them.

Tony Lloyd MP

A nation that has been involved in two major wars and a number of other wars and conflicts in the course of one century ought to remember all those of its citizens who were called upon or even forced to sacrifice their lives.

My earliest memories still include my own father's sadness over many years following the death of his brother in the First World War, a death which ironically was futile as it served very little military purpose. Perhaps at this time more than ever, where once again we see war in Europe and the carnage in Bosnia, it is essential that we remember the terrible suffering and the ultimate futility of war. Remembering the past is one of the best ways of doing this.

Mr Bruce and Mr Lloyd speak of a single loss in their family and the effect this had on those left behind. The carnage of the First World War was such that numerous families lost many of their sons. Very often it was the more established families, land-owners, or those who had a strong voice in industry or parliament who endured the harshest sacrifice. This was the officer class, men who were in the thick of the action, men who led from the front. It is no wonder therefore, that some of our country's leading families lost so many sons. Dame Barbara Cartland and Sir John Gielgud give very moving accounts of their own family losses.

From: Dame Barbara Cartland, D.B.E., D.St.J.

CAMFIELD PLACE,
HATFIELD,
HERTFORDSHIRE.
AL9 6JE

21st January 1994.

My Father was killed in 1918 after surviving four years in the trenches when there was the slaughter of a whole generation of men.

My husband was only eighteen when he was badly wounded at Passchendaele.

He was in hospital for five years and eventually died when he was sixty-two of his war wounds.

My two brothers, Ronald and Anthony were killed at Dunkirk. The eldest Ronald being the first Member of Parliament to have died and Tony who was left to hold back the German advance and on being asked by the Germans three times to surrender. he replied : "I will surrender only unto God."

Naturally I remember all these members of my Family and I have absolute proof that they know I remember them.

It is I think very important for the generation which is growing up to realist the enormous sacrifice that has been made by the men of this century.

We are in this country, only free because they gave their lives for England.

*I am
Barbara Cartland*

Dame Barbara Cartland DBE

My Father was killed in 1918 after surviving four years in the trenches when there was the slaughter of a whole generation of men. My husband was only eighteen when he was badly wounded at Passchendaele. He was in hospital for five years and eventually died when he was sixty-two of his war wounds.

My two brothers, Ronald and Anthony were killed at Dunkirk. The eldest Ronald being the first Member of Parliament to have died and Tony who was left to hold back the German advance and on being asked by the Germans three times to surrender, he replied: "I will surrender only unto God." Naturally I remember all these members of my family and I have absolute proof that they know I remember them.

It is I think very important for the generation which is growing up to realise the enormous sacrifice that has been made by the men of this century. We are in this country, only free because they gave their lives for England.

Two generations (a father and son) killed in two World Wars. Left: Capt. Bertram Cartland APM, taken in 1915; right, Capt. Ronald Cartland, taken on the day before he left for France in January 1940. Ronald was the first Member of Parliament to have been killed in the Second World War. (Photos: courtesy Dame Barbara Cartland)

Sir John Gielgud

I was at preparatory school when the 1914 war broke out, but I remember vividly how shocked we were when the brother of the headmaster, who had also been teaching us a few weeks earlier, was killed. My eldest (and cleverest) brother was very badly wounded and, his life being despaired of, my parents were allowed to visit him in the hospital at Le Touquet, where my mother stayed for several weeks, helping to write letters for the men, while my second brother was training at Bushey when peace came, a day of great excitement and jubilation at Westminster

School, where I had become a scholar. Rationing and zeppelin raids were tedious and unpleasant as well as extremely exhausting for my stockbroker father, who spent long nights as a special constable patrolling the Lots Road factories in Chelsea. My elder brother was invalided out of the army, but was badly crippled, though he joined the Red Cross, for which he laboured throughout his life and insisting on joining the Foreign Office when the Second World War broke out. Several members of my family, both in France and Poland, lost their lives in the First World War, and I could not be unaware of the shadows that seemed always to surround us. Few of us, alas, are left now. How lucky I was to have escaped to live for these many years and to have had the extraordinary good fortune to be able to begin in a peaceful profession that I have so greatly loved and I will never forget the vivid memories I still have of those unforgettable years when so much misery and courageous unselfishness surrounded me on all sides and there were so many tragedies in every family.

Undoubtedly, one of the worst things about losing a dear one in war, must be the fact that they are buried so far away, in some foreign corner. Pilgrimages to war cemeteries and the European battlefields are certainly not uncommon, though they can only be rare luxuries for relatives. This is particularly true of those who perished in the campaigns of the Far East.

Peter Brooke MP

Though members of my immediate family served in the Second World War (my uncle Ken Mathews, who served as an RNVR chaplain on HMS *Norfolk*, in both the *Bismarck* and *Scharnhorst* actions, was unusual as a chaplain in receiving both the OBE and the DSC for gallantry), no member of my immediate family died in the war, and for that I have to go back to the closing weeks of the First World War, when my father's only brother, serving as a navigator in the Royal Flying Corps, was shot down on a reconnaissance flight over Germany at the age of 23.

My grandmother, his mother, lived nearly 40 years after

that and I knew both from her and from my father of the family's sense of loss. I was therefore profoundly moved, when my own brother and I went to look for his grave in a German cemetery (they were buried where they fell), a boy of 13, himself born since the Second World War, immediately asked us whether we had come to see the graves of the English flyers and took us to them unerringly in the town cemetery.

I found that a moving vignette of how war touches both families and communities in a poignant and vivid manner and serves to remind us of what we must always seek to avoid – and of what we owe.

Ann Clwyd MP

A few years ago I was able to visit for the first time the grave of an uncle who died in a Japanese prisoner of war camp during the Second World War. He and hundreds of others are buried in Jakarta, Indonesia.

Before I went, I was interviewed on a BBC Wales programme and as a result of an invitation for others with relatives buried there to contact me, I was asked to visit twelve graves in all and to take photographs.

I placed flowers on the lovingly tended graves and found the experience deeply moving. My uncle was so young, the only son of a farmer. He could have avoided fighting at all. But like so many others, he believed it was his duty.

England might have been a far different place if history had taken another course. Perhaps it seems irrelevant now, 50 years later, but what if we asked ourselves two basic questions. First: What would the world be like if England and Germany had called a truce in 1940? What if our grandparents and parents had gone back to work instead of going to war? It's a hypothetical question but consider the further inhumanities that would have been committed. If England had just carried on regardless would the Nazis have remained in power and would they still be in power today? While we were listening to rock and roll in the 1950s, and the Beatles in the 1960s, would Europe still have been oppressed, would the death camps have maintained an endless reign of terror and blood. Who would have been the next victims of their hatred. Like I say, this is a hypothetical question, as ultimately Hitler made all the wrong political and military moves. His aggression towards Soviet Russia and his Alliance with Japan, which eventually brought the financial and material monster of America down on him, would have undoubtedly severed any agreement, however base, with the United Kingdom. Quite possibly, truce or no truce, Hitler would have set his sights on invading England anway. Hitler's guarantees, guaranteed nothing.

The following are just a few examples of Hitler's public mendacity.

"I wish to work whole-heartedly with England for world peace and do not intend to give offence to anybody if it can be avoided." *February 1933.*

"We do not want war merely for the purpose of bringing to Germany people who simply do not want to be and cannot be Germans. Germany will tread no other path than that laid down by the treaties. The German Government will discuss all political and economic questions only within the framework and through its treaties. The German people have no thought of invading any country." *May 1933.*

"No one could demand that millions of men in the flower of youth should be annihilated for the sake of a readjustment of indefinite scope of our present frontier." *October 1933.*

"I am against war because I am an honest German who, as a soldier, behaved honestly and intends to live so in the future." *November 1933.*

"The German people know no vengeance and wish for no conquest, but would like to take the hand of every other nation." *May 1934.*

"When has the German people ever broken its word?" *November 1934.*

"Among those good things which mankind most earnestly wishes for there can be no doubt that the most fervently desired is world peace . . . . However great the obstacles to peace may be, they can be overcome by the co-operation of all men of good will and with the application of justice and brotherly love, those virtues which are indispensable for world-wide understanding." *January 1935.*

"Germany has reached a non-aggression pact with Poland

which she will keep blindly and which she hopes will be prolonged constantly and will lead to more and more friendly relations . . . . Germany has nothing to gain by a European war. We want peace." *May 1935.*

"Germany will never break the peace of Europe. After three years I can regard the struggle for German equality as concluded today. We have no territorial demands to make in Europe." *March 1936.*

"Germany is an island of peace." *October 1937.*

"I am grateful to Mr. Chamberlain for all his efforts and I have assured him that the German people want nothing but peace . . . I have further assured him, and I emphasize it now, that when this problem (Czechoslovakia) is solved, Germany has no more territorial problems in Europe." *September 1938.*

"Only the warmongers think there will be a war. I think there will be a long period of peace." *January 1939.*

These quotes are picked from a liberal supply, of which, perhaps the most prophetic comes from November 1933: "If I were mad I would want war."

The second question we should ask ourselves is what would have happened if England had lost the war. If the Luftwaffe had overcome the 'Few' in the Battle of Britain and the German army had successfully invaded our home land, what would have become of our cherished freedom? It's not until we examine how fragile a line there was between the success and defeat of the RAF in that summer of 1940 that we realise quite what was at stake, and how much we owe to those gallant pilots who kept the hoards at bay.

So as you can see, when someone talks of the freedom and liberty that we now enjoy, it is a moral crime to take that freedom for granted and an insult to our forefathers when that freedom is questioned.

Ken Livingstone MP

Whatever the argument about the rights or wrongs of Britain's imperial past, no-one can deny that in 1940 the future of civilisation hung in the balance, menaced by the Nazis' evil doctrine of racial purity. Without the determination of the British people to fight on, whatever the cost, most of the world would still be under the

domination of Hitler's heirs and whole races would have
been wiped from the face of our planet. All humankind for
all time owes a debt to those who chose to fight the Nazi
evil. This moment was truly the hinge of humankind's
destiny. The British people and those of so many nations
who rallied to this great cause determined the whole future
of human history.

David Curry MP

I was born just one week after D-Day. I am, therefore, a
child of the liberation and my own freedom was bought
and paid for by the soldiers who secured that victory. Every
year I stand during the Last Post at the ceremonies in the
little towns in my constituency and read the names on the
War Memorials and feel the intensity of those stark and
simple words, 'They shall not grow old . . . ..' It is Britain
renewing her faith with her past and giving thanks for her
future secured by others but up to us to realise.

The other great legacy which the Hero Generation has entrusted
to us, is the unity within Europe itself. Each British serviceman
who took up arms, not only fought for England but for her
European cousins. Our victory and the Nazi defeat was very
much a victory for Germany itself. It is a sad and terrible shame
that while we celebrate this anniversary, in some parts of Europe,
war, tyranny and ethnic cleansing are once again in evidence.
You have only to read the newspapers and watch the television
news to realise how the freedoms which were fought for are now
being abused and disregarded. Once again human beings in
Europe are being subjected to the cruellest and most despicable
inhumanities imaginable. All the more reason again to
appreciate our own liberty and to endeavour, as combined
European nations to find peaceful and dignified solutions to
such wickedness, not only in Europe but throughout the world.

As well as peace within Europe, the war gave Britain itself a
tremendous sense of unity. A unity in which everyone – not just
those in the armed forces – pulled together for victory. This
tremendous national spirit is now very familiar to even our
youngest children, through films and television. They were dark

times, but it was a 'Great Britain.' Mothers queued for their family rations, sisters worked from sunrise to sunset in the fields or munitions factories and grandfathers protected our villages with their Home Guard Platoon.

David Blunkett MP

The spirit of 1945 was not merely a triumph of democracy over totalitarianism and good over evil, but also a rekindling of the desire to work together to create a Britain worth living in.

War inevitably pulled people together and reinforced a sense of interdependence and common purpose. Regaining that spirit today, and reshaping the post-war settlement would be a fitting tribute to those who gave their lives to protect our freedoms, our liberties and our civilisation.

Hopefully the contributions to this book emphasise how the people of Britain made their sacrifices in many different ways, whether on the battle field or here at home. People in Britain were asked to do charitable things and the nation's charity was boundless. Dame Catherine Cookson and Marjorie Proops relate their own experiences as war wives.

Dame Catherine Cookson DBE

I was eight years old when the First World War started; and I remember it through my Uncle Jack who, one night in 1914, got drunk and woke up to find he and his pal were in the army, having signed on the previous evening and received the King's shilling.

He was killed in 1918, two months before Armistice. I have a photograph of his grave in France.

My memory of the Second World War is more vivid. I had a large house, and Hastings in 1939 was, if you can believe it, a reception area. I had been ordered to take in twelve blind women evacuees from London. In fact, what the coach deposited in my drive was twelve blind men from

The grave of Lance
Corporal J. McMullen,
(Dame Catherine
Cookson's uncle Jack)
Durham Light
Infantry, in the
Abbeville Cemetery
France.
(Photo courtesy Dame
Catherine Cookson)

the East End of London. The consequent events of the
following year would fill a number of books, but one stands
out: on Saturday, 1st June 1940 I was married. We were to
make our way to Grays, Essex, for a one-night honeymoon.
The train stopped at Tunbridge Wells, and I saw the sight
that was to stay with me until now: the train at the opposite
platform was disgorging French soldiers, all seeming to be
wearing the same expression in their faces, one which I can
describe only as a mixture of bitterness, anger, and
hopelessness. The effect on me was to cry for the
remainder of the journey to London, with the result that I
bled profusely from the hereditary telangiectases in my
nose.

The last distinct memory, for me, of that war was the day
my husband was demobbed and returned to our time-
bombed badly damaged home.

Marjorie Proops OBE

I, like so many young women of my age at the time, was the wife of a serving soldier. My late husband was in the Royal Engineers, serving in the Far East. During the four years he served, he had no home leave and indeed became a remote figure, despite our daily exchange of letters.

Life was very tough for a war wife, working in London, dodging bombs in the blitz, bringing up a baby, fearful always for that baby's safety. During that period I was a freelance artist living in Stoke Poges but going to London nearly every day to deliver drawings to newspapers and magazines, and certain that when I got home to my small boy, the house where we had a bed-sit would have been demolished by a bomb. In fact we did have one bomb through the roof but, luckily, no one was hurt.

But despite the constant anxiety and danger, my lasting memory of that period of my life was the fantastic camaraderie of the people of London, the support we all gave each other, the amazing humour bubbling up through the fear.

No one would want a war again to get people to be nice to each other. Isn't it sad that it had to take a war to prove that they can be?

When we consider the act of Remembrance in the way it is celebrated in Britain, we must also consider the millions of Europeans who died as our allies. We must appreciate that they are free to remember or not as they see fit. In many ways, and sadly, the whole question of Remembrance in terms of European unity is becoming more and more delicate, here emphasised by Norman Lamont.

Norman Lamont MP

I was amazed and horrified when President Giscard d'Estaing proposed that France should abolish all ceremonies commemorating victory over Germany in the Second World War.

I understand why, in the interests of complete European

unity, he held this view but I felt it was profoundly wrong.

There are two reasons why we need to remember the Second World War and should never forget it. Firstly, we need to remember the individuals and their names because we owe so much to them. Secondly, peace cannot be taken for granted, it has to be worked for. Those who died gave us peace for many years.

John MacGregor OBE MP

In my constituency of South Norfolk, there are a great many veterans of the two world wars, a large proportion of whom served in the Far East during the Second World War, experiencing some of the most bitter conflicts of the war. Their valiant struggles must not be forgotten.

I never fail to be moved by a Remembrance Day Service. I have been privileged several times to attend the Service at the Cenotaph in Whitehall, the focal point of the nation's mourning and remembrance. It is equally moving, and possibly more poignant, to attend the services in our towns and small villages, as I do in Norfolk, where people are still remembered personally.

The memory of two World Wars is one of the things which drives me to appreciate and value the close ties we now have across the international divide and especially with our partners in the European Union.

I have spent much of my 12 years as a Government Minister negotiating in Brussels on everyday issues. How vital it is that we now settle our differences, however great or small, around the table and not across the battle field.

Those who gave their lives in the two World Wars in order that future generations could live in freedom and harmony did not die in vain.

50 years is a long time ago and each year on Remembrance Sunday, towns and villages up and down the country take part in one of our great annual traditions. But with each new ceremony, the old soldiers grow older, the remaining heroes grow less, 'The Few' get fewer, and their stories and memories become ever more faint.

Lord Carrington

The Second World War happened a long time ago. You have to be 70 or so to have participated, and memories are fast fading, but not to those who fought in it. There are many who are still suffering from the wounds and experiences that they had at that time. I hope this Book will do something to remind some people of the debts they still owe to those still living.

As we celebrate this Anniversary another very important question we have to ask ourselves is what does the future have in store. The participation of World War combatants at each Remembrance parade is an established tradition, but one day the last of the old soldiers, sailors and airmen will have gone and their memories with them. As Lord Carrington points out, to have fought in the Second World War you would have to be 70. Every year the blank file in the ranks increases and the roll call is left more and more unanswered. What will happen in these towns and villages up and down the country when the last old soldier has gone. What will become of Remembrance Sunday, will it simply cease to exist?

Sir Cyril Smith MBE LLD(Hon) DL

I strongly believe that Remembrance Sunday should continue, and I personally have stood at the Rochdale Cenotaph for 44 continuous years on each of these days.

I see this Remembrance not as glorifying war, but as reminding us of the scourge of it. We think of those who gave their all, of those, too, who were disabled by war, and of families left to carry the emotional (not to mention material) burden of the consequences.

The Royal British Legion do a wonderful work. Remembrance Day is their day – but it is also OUR day – our day to remember, our day to remind ourselves, and our day to remind our successors. There are no winners in war – only losers. That is the message of our Remembrance. Let us never forget it or fail to take the opportunity to ensure we do not do so.

Sir Cyril Smith, M.B.E., L.L.D.(Hon), D.L.

[Handwritten note, transcribed below in print:]

Of course Remembrance Sunday should continue, long after the last living participants have gone. We should never be allowed to forget the debt that we owe. Never take for granted the freedoms that we have discussed and never undervalue the strength of the lasting peace that was created.

It is our heritage as members of the Royal British Legion to secure the continuation of Remembrance Sunday.

Richard Ryder MP

The Royal British Legion must be sustained by each generation to remind men and women all over the country of the need to honour the heroes of our past battles for liberty as well as our duty to guard the peace by maintaining our defences.

If Remembrance Sunday is to continue long into the future, the job will fall on the shoulders of the younger generations. It is our duty to guard and cherish our history and learn from its lessons, so that the act of Remembrance remains as much a part of the future as a thing of the past.

Dame Vera Lynn DBE

Knowing my connections with the Armed Services I am always being asked "Should we still have Remembrance Day?", and I am always surprised that anyone should ask this.

It is vital that we all remember those who gave their lives for us and what better way is there than Remembrance Day?

I do wish the children and young people were more involved in this special day. I would like to see in this country what happens in Holland. Every child at some point in their school years places flowers on the graves of our British boys who died there. In this way they will always remember that special day and what it means.

Let us show their families and loved ones they left behind that we have not forgotten their sacrifice and that we will remember them.

Dame Vera Lynn is one of a unique group of people the mention of who's name inevitably makes us think of the Second World War.
(Photo coutesy Dame Vera Lynn).

Sir Norman Fowler MP

Every November the Fields of Remembrance are set out meticulously in the churchyard alongside Westminster Abbey and St Margaret's. It is particularly moving to walk through that part of Westminster then and remember how much we owe to the men and women who sacrificed their lives in two world wars, and since then, in the service of our country.

I attend the Remembrance Sunday Service in my constituency of Sutton Coldfield where we gather to remember those who lost their lives from our local community. Some may say that our act of Remembrance is no longer of relevance to young generations who have no recollection of war. I personally could not disagree with that view more and we should not forget that so many of those who gave their lives were young men and women with their future ahead of them.

The Royal British Legion is one of Britain's finest organisations and continues its vital role in looking after current and retired service men and women, their families and dependents. I am delighted to be associated with this particular project to mark the 50th Anniversary of the end of the Second World War, and to support such a worthwhile cause.

Having served with No 4626 Aeromedical Evacuation Squadron of the Royal Auxiliary Air Force based at RAF Lyneham in Wiltshire, the author is very much aware of the daily coming and going of Hercules aircraft to all corners of the world where people are in need of relief and humanitarian aid. No 4626 Squadron had the distinction to be the only Auxiliary unit since the end of the Second World War to have been mobilised and sent on active service. This took place in the 1991 Gulf War when the whole squadron was sent to various locations within Saudi Arabia, Oman and Abu Dhabi. The Gulf War and humanitarian missions to the former Yugoslavia are only a few examples of how British servicemen still uphold the traditions which those who fought in the two World Wars established; the fight for freedom. This then is their legacy to us, the legacy of liberation. The experiences of today will form the basis of our Remembrance for the future.

Michael Heseltine MP

This is, indeed, a time for remembrance. Remembrance, not of victory, but of the longed-for ending of the hostilities which had torn Europe apart for six weary years and of, as King George VI put it at the time, our "safe deliverance" as a nation from all the horrors of the Second World War.

All of us alive today – even those born long after the war was over – are in a very real sense the survivers of that dreadful experience. For out of that war grew the determination, shared by men and women throughout Western Europe, to spare no effort to ensure that it should never happen again. Thanks to that commitment and dedication we can also remember today 50 years of peace.

But it is a time, too, for us to remember those who did not survive the conflict. And that is as it should be. We must never allow ourselves to take for granted those who died. Their sacrifice secured for the generations that came after the chance to live and work to build that peace – in freedom. Their life for ours. That is a debt we can never fully repay. But we can remember.

Paul Scofield

Horace 65–8 BC.
"Non Omnis moriar."
"I shall not altogether die."
Written so long ago, the words still ring for us. Forgetting is altogether dying.

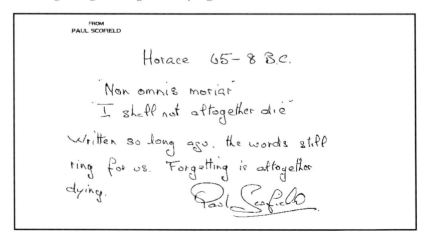

CHAPTER TWO

THE HERO GENERATION

In this chapter the Hero Generation of 1939–1945 give their own views on the subject of Remembrance. These were the men who actually fought the battles and participated in these great events, on land, sea or in the air. However modest they may appear, each is a hero, and representative of the millions who served alongside them. In putting together this book I have deliberately approached characters of high esteem and rank. Many of you reading this book will undoubtedly know people who served during the Second World War and who are just as deserving of a mention. All I can do is to emphasise the fact that they were all heroes, and my choice of contributors was based on people I felt to be representative of their country or their service. A number of people I approached were unable to contribute due to ill health, and this in itself, brings home to us all, just how appropriate a time it is to pay homage to their ever depleting ranks. In other parts of the book you may read the thoughts of people who also served during the war but who are not listed in this chapter. They are no less part of the Hero Generation, but their contributions to the Book of Remembrance better fit other sections. Represented here are heroes from the Army, the Royal Air Force and the Royal Navy; VCs, MCs and DFCs, and those of more modest participation, on the Home Front or helping to keep our war machine in operation. The Golden Book of Remembrance is dedicated to their friends and comrades who are not here today to write their own thoughts, and whose everlasting spirit they represent.

Sir Edward Heath KG MBE MP

In August 1939, I set out from Dover to hitch-hike across Europe to Danzig, then the centre of dispute between Germany and Poland. This trip across Europe, carried out just before the outbreak of hostilities, enabled me to visit many splendid cities including Dusseldorf, Berlin, Warsaw, Leipzig, Strasbourg and Paris. It brought home to me that

Bill Reid V.C.

24th January '94.

<u>50th Anniversary of the end of the Second World War.</u>

Over the years I have often been asked how I feel about my award of the Victoria Cross.

In the action which resulted in my award — we were flying back from the target when all four engines cut out over the Channel. This was because of the injuries to our Crew, and damage to the aircraft; we had been fully involved in keeping the 'plane flying on the correct heading, and had omitted to maintain the fuel balance in the tanks. The Flight Engineer corrected this by switching over the tanks and the engines restarted.

We had virtually completed the action which was to result in the award of the Victoria Cross, other than land the 'plane somewhere in England,

Had we gone down in the Channel — our story would never have been told. How many times must this have happened to other crews, sailors + soldiers

2/ in action. I feel therefore, that it has been awarded for all those who were unable to tell their own stories. In remembering this 50th Anniversary, I also take pride in the achievements of the American Airmen, who were our partners & comrades in arms & mourn their losses as we do our own. In June 1992, I attended the "Gathering of Eagles" at Maxwell ~~Field~~ Air Force Base, Montgomery, Alabama. During the week I attended a Memorial was unveiled to:

1st Lt. Karl D. Richter
Killed in action — July 28th 1967 — North Vietnam

The inscription, by A.E. Houseman, I feel could apply to all airmen who have made the supreme sacrifice. It reads:

Here dead lie we, because we did not choose
To live, and shame the land from which we spring
Life, to be sure, is nothing much to lose
But young men think it is, and we were young.

Bill Reid V.C.
61&617 Squadrons RAFVR.
Bomber Command.

the Europe through which I journeyed was soon to be ravaged by war.

When I fought across Europe in 1944 and 1945 whilst serving with the Royal Artillery, I witnessed at first-hand the destruction, carnage and misery of modern warfare. Cities across the continent were razed to the ground. Europe had once again destroyed itself.

The devastation and despair which surrounded the Allied armies as they made their way across a shattered Europe was to make a tremendous impact on all of us involved.

Confronted with such scenes, I became convinced of the deep belief that remains with me to this day: that the peoples of Europe must never again be allowed to fight each other. We can only hope that by remembering all those who made the ultimate sacrifice, future generations may be able to grasp firmly the ideals of peace and reconciliation.

Bill Reid VC

Over the years I have often been asked how I feel about my award of the Victoria Cross.

In the action which resulted in my award, we were flying back from the target when all four engines cut out over the Channel. This was because of the injuries to our crew, and damage to the aircraft; we had been fully involved in keeping the plane flying on the correct heading, and had omitted to maintain the fuel balance in the tanks. The Flight Engineer corrected this by switching over the tanks and the engines restarted.

We had virtually completed the action which was to result in the award of the Victoria Cross, other than land the plane somewhere in England.

Had we gone down in the Channel, our story would never have been told. How many times must this have happened to other crews, sailors and soldiers in action. I feel therefore, that it has been awarded for all those who were unable to tell their own stories.

In remembering this 50th Anniversary, I also take pride in the achievements of the American Airmen, who were our partners and comrades in arms and mourn their losses as we do our own. In June 1992, I attended the 'Gathering of Eagles' at Maxwell Air Force Base, Montgomery, Alabama. During the week I attended a memorial was unveiled to: 1st Lt. Karl D. Richter killed in action 28 July 1967, North Vietnam. The inscription, by A.E. Houseman, I feel could apply to all airmen who have made the supreme sacrifice. It reads: 'Here dead lie we, because we did not choose to live, and shame the land from which we sprung. Life, to be sure, is nothing much to lose. But young men think it is, and we were young.'

HARRY SECOMBE

When I was a lad, the two minutes silence on Armistice Day, November 11th, were strictly observed. Nothing stirred during that time on the eleventh hour of the eleventh day of the eleventh month. The war was still fresh in people's minds in the 20's and early 30's and too many mantlepieces in the little parlours on the council estate on which we lived held framed photographs of stiffly posed soldiers who never came back. It was easy to remember then.

Later on, the event seemed to have less significance to me as a teenager. It was a time for older people to remember and the names on the Cenotaph struck no cord in me. When the next war drew near, I was eager to be part of it and joined the Territorial Army. I never regretted doing so because Hitler was an evil man and had to be stopped. At the same time, looking back, if the whole world had been forced to stop and think, would we have had to fight again?

Today, I can put faces to the names on the War Memorial; fresh young faces full of promise for a future denied them. That is why our youngsters must remember before they, too, fall into the trap of forgetfulness.

Harry Secombe

SIR HARRY SECOMBE CBE

Sir Harry Secombe CBE

When I was a lad, the two minutes silence on Armistice Day, November 11th, were strictly observed. Nothing stirred during that time on the eleventh hour of the eleventh day of the eleventh month. The war was still fresh in people's minds in the 20's and early 30's and too many mantlepieces in the little parlours on the council estate on which we lived held framed photographs of stiffly posed soldiers who never came back. It was easy to remember then.

Later on, the event seemed to have less significance to me as a teenager. It was a time for older people to remember and the names on the Cenotaph struck no cord in me. When the next war drew near, I was eager to be part of it and joined the Territorial Army. I never regretted doing so because Hitler was an evil man and had to be stopped. At the same time, looking back, if the whole world had been forced to stop and think, would we have had to fight again?

Today, I can put faces to the names on the War Memorial; fresh young faces full of promise for a future denied them. That is why our youngsters must remember before they, too, fall into the trap of forgetfulness.

*Actor Michael Denison taken at the time of being commissioned as 2nd Lieutenant in the Intelligence Corps in 1941.
(Photo courtesy Michael Denison)*

MICHAEL DENISON C.B.E.

I was born in 1915, living in Richmond Surrey with an uncle and aunt, my mother having died in child-birth. My earliest recollections were of the Star and Garter Home being built and of wounded ex-servicemen, dressed, if memory serves, in sort of blue pyjamas.

My uncle – a Boer War mounted trooper, who was prevented by his employer from enlisting in WW I – had an office in Whitehall directly overlooking the Cenotaph; and we always attended the Armistice Day Service. The last time I did so was on 11 November 1938 taking my best friend from school (who was to be my best man the next year and be killed in the Normandy landings) After the Service I went and proposed to my wife and was accepted; Remembrance Day has been an easy day to remember!

During WW II I served six years in the Army at home and overseas, and though not a military man by inclination, and inevitably missing my profession, I hope I made some worthwhile contribution.

It was evil things we were fighting against, and even if not all were defeated – how could they be? – the sacrifices of life, or limb, or youth must be cherished, not forgotten.

Michael Denison

Michael Denison CBE

I was born in 1915, living in Richmond Surrey with an uncle and aunt, my mother having died in child-birth. My earliest recollections were of the Star and Garter Home being built and of wounded ex-servicemen, dressed, if memory serves, in sort of blue pyjamas.

My uncle – a Boer War mounted trooper, who was prevented by his employer from enlisting in the First World War – had an office in Whitehall directly overlooking the Cenotaph; and we always attended the Armistice Day Service. The last time I did so was on 11 November 1938, taking my best friend from school (who was to be my best man a year later and then killed in the Normandy landings). After the service I went and proposed to my wife and was accepted; Remembrance Day has been an easy day to remember!

During the Second World War I served for six years in the army at home and overseas, and though not a military man by inclination, and inevitably missing my profession, I hope I made some worthwhile contribution. We were fighting against evil things, and even if not all were defeated – how could they be? – the sacrifices of life, or limb, or youth must be cherished, not forgotten.

Patrick Moore CBE

I was born in 1923. My father served in the trenches during the First World War; in the process he collected an MC, but also collected a lungful of poison gas, and was never really fit again. During the Second World War I flew as a navigator with RAF Bomber Command (candour compels me to admit that when I applied for aircrew training and was asked my age, I was somewhat economical with the truth).

Between 1939 and 1945 we were fighting against the most evil regime that the world has ever known; those who have been born since that time, and depend upon what they read in books and see on television, seldom appreciate how appalling it was. There are also some people who set out to belittle what was done. We won the war; on neither occasion did the United States join the conflict until the worst was over. We threw away the peace, which means that if the worst happens we may have to fight for a third time.

I was lucky; I emerged more or less unscathed, but many others did not, so do not forget those Britons who gave their lives or their health so that our planet was not taken over by pure evil.

Hammond Innes

Dawn just breaking and the start of the assault only minutes away. I was a gunner captain who had switched to British Army Newspapers. I ran a syndication office feeding articles to our nine editions spread over four countries and was on a Landing Craft (G) approaching the French coast. The (G) stood for GUN, an ancient naval three-inch mounted in the tank hold.

Away on our starb'd beam, the mighty *Richelieu*, flagship of the French fleet, was a dark silhouette, her guns swinging towards the northern horizon where the villas of the Côte d'Azur drew a sharp white line. I had talked my way on to this venture via the C-in-C Med and now I was rather wishing I had not, for we had opened our orders. These were to give close support to the first wave of assault craft and silence any opposition.

As soon as we read that we all of us grabbed for the wardroom first aid book! The words Close Support meant we would be a sitting duck when it was daylight. One 88 . . .

Oh to be on the *Richelieu*. The Free French were going home. They were flying a tricolour half a block long and they were cheering as the first wave of assault craft creamed past them. Moments later the whole fleet opened up, pounding the shore as the light grew.

But there were no 88s, no opposition – the Germans had backed off, and I was left thinking what it must be like for the Free French, their home-land at last, and no opposition.

Some years later, driving south in search of spring sunshine, in that year when the Bouche de Rhone froze over, we stopped at Chateauneuf-du-Pape. Waiting for our meal Chez la Mère Germaine, relaxed and passing the time drinking the red stuff warmly steaming in brandy glasses, Dorothy found the Visitors' Book. She turned automatically to the period just after the fall of France and called me over to read page after page of heartbreaking, poignant scribbling, a record so unexpected – signature after signature, most with their rank and their regiment – all the famous ones, and some we had never heard of. Vive la France. Those words again and again.

It was the bravest, most pathetic document I have ever read, cream of a great nation fleeing south to the Mediterranean to fight again from Africa. The desperate hopes, messages to loved ones, to comrades feared dead – messages to friends who might just possibly pass this way.

Reading these brief, sad, sometimes violent epistles was a glimpse into the heart of men in defeat, some wounded, most near to despair, yet still determined to fight on.

We sat over our meal, sad and silent, except for the occasional comment on what it must have been like hiding and running and starving, families and friends abandoned – and all in order to fight again.

Vive la France.

I told Dorothy then about the *Richelieu* and that enormous great tricolour and the cheer that went up as the barrage started and the assault craft roared away.

This is a glimpse of another country's travail. The Cenotaph and all those village war memorials throughout Britain bear testimony in the name of our dead to what it cost to keep our country free. But France was occupied and the roll of the dead contains many who kept faith with their comrades and died under torture.

Pause then at France's memorials, the long string of names, particularly in the area of the massif Central where the Resistance was most active.

Oh God, may our children be taught to understand what it cost to have the freedom they possess, the freedom to speak their minds without fear. Freedom seems such a simple matter when you have it, but when it is taken from you . . . .!

Peter Malam Brothers, who flew Hurricanes during the Battle of Britain, destroyed 15 enemy aircraft and won the DSO, DFC and bar. He remained in the Royal Air Force after the war, and attained the rank of Air Commodore.
(Photo coutesy Peter Malam Brothers)

Air Commodore Peter M. Brothers CBE DSO DFC

Born towards the end of the First World War I grew up to hear some tales of the horrors and experiences endured by my uncles during their time in the trenches. Also I read and admired the stories of the famous fighter pilots of those early days of aviation, tales of valour which had a romantic flavour for an impressionable young boy; thus were sown the seeds which determined me upon a career in the Royal Air Force.

My father, believing this to be but a passing whim, for my sixteenth birthday gave me a flying course which I used to the full and followed-up by joining the Royal Air Force on his birthday, 27th January 1936.

I had the good fortune to be selected for duty as a fighter pilot and by late 1936 joined No. 32 Squadron at Biggin Hill and saw action throughout the Battle of Britain until rested in December 1940, returning to the fray mid-1941 until, with some rest breaks, the end of hostilities.

Inevitably I lost many good friends and acquaintances and witnessed scenes of horror which can never be erased from my mind. Since the end of the Second World War there has been a succession of wars, Korea and Vietnam to name but two, and many minor conflicts, all of which have brought their trail of devastation and suffering.

Despite the hopes and prayers for peace by people the world over we live in uncertain and dangerous times. By remembering those who made the supreme sacrifice, by remembering the devastation, the pain, suffering and loss of loved ones, these memories can play a major part in bringing about the peace for which all except the evil long.

Colonel P.A. Porteous VC

When I was a small boy at day school, on Armistice Day (11th November) we were taken to church and the Village Memorial at Fleet. We remembered all the local men who had died in the First World War 1914–18. After a short service, we observed the 2 minute silence. In those days, all over the country, traffic stopped, men removed their hats and everyone stood in silent remembrance of the million men killed in that War. The ceremony continues to this day, but, with the passing of the years since the Second World War, memories have faded and young people who were not born during either war are not sure what Remembrance Sunday is all about.

After being awarded my Victoria Cross in 1942, I was asked to talk to schools, factories, the Home Guard etc., about the Dieppe Raid. On one occasion, I was speaking to my old school, Wellington College. The boys in the audience were of all ages and when I looked at the older ones, I wondered how many would survive to see the end of the War. Already so many of my friends had died and many more would, before the end. I wished with all my heart that this could be the last major confrontation.

Since 1945, there have been several minor and major wars – over 400 men in my own Regiment, the Royal Artillery, have been killed. However, I still hope that somehow Peace will finally prevail.

The pilots of 626 (Bomber) Squadron are briefed before an operation over Berlin on December 16th/17th 1943. To learn what happened next, on a similar occasion, see what Michael Bentine has to say.
(Photo courtesy The Wickenby Register)

Michael Bentine

Copyright Michael Bentine 1994

I must confess: "When I remember some parts of my service life, I get a hot flush!!"

For instance: In the winter of 1943, I was an intelligence officer, with 626 and 12 Squadrons, on an operational bomber station, at Wickenby, in Lincolnshire!

One night! All Hell broke loose!

En route to Berlin, our Lancasters met an unexpected gale, and arrived late over the target! The 'Flak' was murderous, and German night-fighters were everywhere.

After barely making it back to base, one of our top pilots, an Australian, was blazing mad. He told me to get him group headquarters on the phone.

My WAAF telephone operator, by mistake, connected me to the war-room at Bomber Command!

Unaware of this, I handed the phone over to the angry Aussie, but stayed on the extension to monitor the call.

He really let rip!!

"Whoever planned this bloody operation should be bloody court-martialed!! It was a monumental cock-up! The weather was bloody murder over target. What the Hell do you morons think you are bloody doing?"

An ice-cold voice answered him:

"Do you know to whom you are speaking?"

"No! And I don't bloody well care, Mate!"

"This is Air Chief Marshal, Sir Arthur Harris, Commander in Chief Bomber Command!!"

For a moment, there was dead silence! Then the shaken Aussie croaked hoarsely:

"Do you know who you are talking to, Sir?"

"No! I don't"

The Aussie muttered: "Thank Christ for that!" and slammed down the phone.

It wasn't blasphemy! He really meant it!!

The next day, there was a hell of a row! And someone came from Command. Naturally, none of us knew a thing about it!

Sir Alec Guinness

I have a gut feeling that some of the ills that attend the nation today stem from the abandonment of the two minute silence of Armistice Day on whichever weekday November 11th occurs. There was something awe inspiring and emotionally charged about all traffic coming to a stand-still, people stopping dead in their tracks as eleven o'clock sounded and the sad silence fell, it seemed forever, on the whole country. Commerce and the rush of things were put in their rightful places as very secondary considerations when compared with the respect and sorrow for the millions of war dead. Turning the ceremony at The Cenotaph into a convenient service on a quiet Sunday morning, impressive as it is, has not the same forthrightness and sense of binding the nation together that the old Armistice Day had.

Raymond Baxter

During the six years 1939–45 the British people were more closely united than at any time in their history. Reluctantly, knowing all too well the appalling consequences, they – we – had gone to war. Unlike the enemy our purpose was neither territorial gain nor political domination. We went to war in defence of our fundamental values – Parliamentary democracy, the rights of the individual within the Law, free speech, religious tolerance – all that we had been taught from early childhood. And what childhood we had enjoyed. Certainly there was poverty and unemployment. But no violence accompanied the Jarrow Marchers; children were safe to wander the countryside alone, ride their bicycles to school, and pop down to the corner shop on errands in the dark.

Nor, when we went to war, were we alone. From September 3rd 1939, the peoples of the Empire and Commonwealth rallied in support of what they regarded as the Mother Country. Long before their own homelands came under threat from Imperial Japan, and the United States was drawn into the war, the Australians and New Zealanders were, like the Canadians, following the example of their fathers twenty-five years before. The South African Air Force was speedily in action, and units of the Indian Army embarked for France. From the sun-kissed islands of the Caribbean volunteers were soon flying with the Royal Air Force and ex-patriots from the world over abandoned the security of their lives abroad to join His Majesty's Forces.

So they – we – fought the Second World War – on land, sea and in the air; in the factories and the shipyards; in the fields and down the mines. On the Home Front, the children were evacuated, returned and evacuated again. There was no such thing as home leave for the men who left their families for the Western Desert, and later the Far East. Everything was rationed but such 'black-marketing' as sprang up was little more than a game. Many in 'reserved occupations' volunteered as Air Raid Wardens, the Home Guard or other auxiliary services. Housewives joined the WVS, grannies knitted socks and led the sing-songs in the shelters; grandpas went back to work and dug their allotments.

Conscientious Objectors were given a fair hearing and many served with gallantry as ambulance-men and other non combatant roles.

Of course it was far from perfection. Some people made a lot of money. Some gained ill-deserved promotion and decoration. Some went on strike. Some demonstrated to 'Stop the War' or 'Open the Second Front Now.' But they were not sent to the gas-chambers. They were not even interned. In any case, they were an insignificant minority.

In the Second World War the people of Britain fought united in a common cause. They continued to fight despite hardship and heartbreak. They continued to fight when, by all the odds, defeat stared them in the face. They continued to fight and refused to compromise until the very last moment – the unconditional surrender of those who had threatened them.

The price of that victory is incalculable. Numbers are irrelevant. How are the dead to be counted? Is the death of an innocent child in Coventry to be equated with that of a school-boy fighter pilot in the Battle of Britain; the private soldier who died in Malaya, having never seen his fourth child, to the young nurse drowned in a Hospital ship; the Colonel leading his men to the Padre; the cook to the Captain of a submarine?

Sacrifice is equal and indivisible. Remembrance – and re-dedication – is our common obligation.

Sir Christopher Cockerell CBE
The Engines of War
Copyright Sir Christopher Cockerell 1994

War was declared on Germany on 3rd September 1939. We all knew what it was about. It was a people's war. We were all in it, men and women, whether we were soldiers or Administrators, or Nurses, or in industry, or on the land. Perhaps my own experiences typifies what was happening all over the country, for we hadn't nearly enough of the 'Engines of War' – Destroyers, Freighters, Aircraft, Tanks, Guns, Trucks, Submarines, Uniforms and a thousand other things. On October 20th 1939, a Wing-Commander from Bomber Command came down to Marconi's at Writtle, near Chelmsford, to visit my section, which was responsible for the development of aircraft equipment. We went out to lunch and he told me that Bomber Command was not satisfied with the new Communication and Navigation equipment that the Royal Aircraft Establishment had designed for them, and what could Marconi's suggest? Having no paper handy, I pulled a used envelope from my pocket, and wrote out a specification of an equipment to fulfill their requirements; and the next day we got the word to go. My section was housed in some old wooden ex-Army huts.

After discussing the Transmitter with George Parker, my second-in-command, then, with two colleagues, Brailsford and Cufflin, I went to E.K. Cole's at Southend, who knew more about line production than we in Marconi's did. Their Chief Engineer, Hunt, lent me his office and Lab., and Shackleton, his Head Draughtsman in the Drawing Office, and we set about designing the Receiver and Navigation Units. We devised a visual method of checking that the aircraft was flying on the correct and not the reciprocal of the correct bearing; and a visual method using crossed needles to enable the pilot to fly on course – soon to be known as the 'Drunken Men'. The Transmitter was designed with click-stop tuning, permitting quick changes of frequency; and to be capable of operating in the rarefied air at high altitudes. We worked seven days a week to about 10p.m. and had Christmas Day off, and had a complete equipment installed in a bomber on January 5th 1940, exactly eleven weeks after the start. Everyone helped. The tests were O.K. We were all exhausted. The equipments were being installed in quantity in June of that year. 125,000 equipments were made, and they cost £4,000 a time, at the start.

Later in the war, George Parker produced a Beacon which was fitted to our aircraft-carriers, to enable the pilots to home in to their carrier. The next job was the Display Unit for the Navy's Long-range Radar; and when this was finished, the last major job was a contract from the Telecommunications Research Establishment to design a device called 'Bagful', which was fitted to our bombers (and some U.S. bombers) and which recorded on a drum the signals from enemy Radar Stations around the coasts of France and Germany and Norway in such a way that the

A tradesman works on TX/RX 1154/55 in a Short Sunderland aircraft of Coastal Command in August 1942. This was one of many vital pieces of equipment designed by Christopher Cockerell and his section at Marconi.
(Crown copyright/MOD. Reproduced with the permission of the Controller of HMSO)

RAF knew the exact positions of the stations and bombed them to extinction just before D-Day, so that the enemy had no 'eyes' to detect our ships or aircraft.

A piece rather like the above could be written about many other endeavours during the war, because it was a constant battle to keep our 'engines of war' as good or better than those of the enemy, and to back up our chaps at the front line – better tanks, better anti-tank guns, aircraft, radar, and longer-range aircraft for Coastal Command – to help win the Battle of the Atlantic, and reduce the terrible losses suffered by our merchant seamen.

Certain people should be mentioned who had a profound effect on the war. Camm, (later Sir Sydney Camm) who designed the 'easy-to-build' Hurricane fighter, which shot down more enemy aircraft than all the other devices and aircraft put together. Rolls-Royce, who as a private venture produced the Merlin aircraft engine, which powered our fighters and bombers and tanks and coastal craft, and saw us through the war. Lady Houston, who financed our Schneider Trophy Supermarine S6 seaplanes, which won the Schneider Trophy outright in 1931, but more importantly, gave R.J. Mitchell the experience to design the Spitfire fighter. Watson-Watt, (later Sir Robert Watson-Watt) of the National Physical Laboratory, who talked, and talked, and finally persuaded the Air Ministry to believe in Radar and to have built a string of Radar stations around our coasts. Without Radar we should have lost the Battle of Britain.

Very early in the war, on November 23rd 1939, a German 'pocket battleship', the *Deutschland*, attacked the civil liner *Rawalpindi*, which only had 4-inch guns. The *Rawalpindi* under Captain Kennedy and with a crew of merchant seamen and naval reservists, went down with all her guns firing and her colours flying. Then I knew, we all knew, that our men had the determination and the sticking-power and the sense of duty that their forebears had at Trafalgar and Waterloo and the ghastly trench warfare of the First World War.

The whole country was put on a war footing. It was for real.

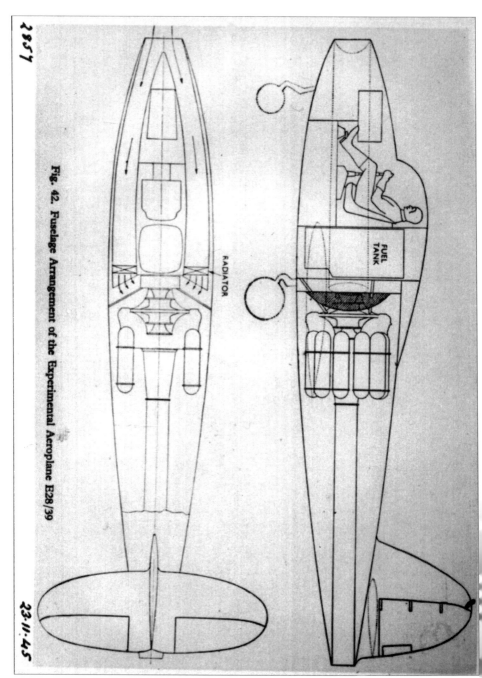

The original plans of the Gloster E28/39 experimental aircraft referred to by Dr G Feilden. This gives a good idea of the novelty of Sir Frank Whittle's concept of a jet aircraft, when compared with the contemporary Hurricane and Spitfire.
(Courtesy Dr G Feilden)

Dr G Feilden CBE

Sir Frank Whittle became interested in the possibilities of jet propulsion when he was a cadet at Cranwell in 1928, and he took out his first Patent in 1930. Official indifference, combined with the depression, prevented him from making any progress with his ideas until 1935 when two brother officers, who had been invalided out of the Royal Air Force, raised sufficient private capital for the ordering of a first experimental engine based on Whittle's designs. This ran in April 1937, and ultimately led to the Air Ministry taking a serious interest in Whittle's proposals. By 1939, an experimental aircraft known as the E28/39, now in the Science Museum, South Kensington, had been ordered from the Gloster Aircraft Company and two engines to power it from the British Thomson-Houston Company in Rugby.

After many problems had been overcome, the airframe and engine were ready for taxiing trials in April 1941. Whittle had appointed me to take charge of the engine installation and I stayed several days in Gloucestershire for this purpose: I was 24 at that time and I felt my responsibility very seriously.

The installation of the engine in the aircraft was completed on the afternoon of 7 April 1941 and the aircraft was taken out on to the grass airfield which was sodden from recent rain. The engine started perfectly, but at 13,000 rpm which we used that afternoon, the aircraft would only taxi at about 20 mph. Everyone was disappointed with this result, but as it was near the end of the day no further attempts were made. The following day, the airfield had dried out, and the engine was allowed to run up to 15,000 rpm. Whittle did some test runs himself, and was very gratified with the simplicity, silence and controlability of the aircraft. The Gloster Chief Test Pilot, Mr P E G Sayer then took over and the engine speed limit was progressively raised to 16,000 rpm at which setting the aircraft made a short flight of about 200 yards, after which it landed, taxied back and repeated the performance twice more. Everyone was delighted with this result, which was followed by ten hours of very successful experimental flying at RAF Cranwell the following month. During these flight trials practically no adjustments were required to either the engine or the airframe. This must be one of the major engineering achievements of this century, in that we were dealing with a revolutionary new system of propulsion, with its engine, and an entirely new form of airframe.

Donald Pleasence

First published in the Battle of Britain 50th Anniversary Brochure

A blue sky. Burning, the aeroplane had fallen away – I could see no other parachute, although I knew I was the only one to jump. I was very lonely, very frightened. I think I had pulled the cord too soon. My parachute had caught on the fuselage and I was going down too fast (it seemed to me). Little puffs of smoke exploded all around. They had got rid of the aeroplane and were having a go at me.

Until some minutes before, I had been a WOP/AG in a Lancaster bomber. This means 'Wireless Operator, Air Gunner'. The daylight operation was unusual. We normally flew at night at high altitudes and without pressurization. Communication between crew members was by radio mike, and sometimes these would mist over and freeze up. It was my job to protect the crew's microphones, and I did this with thin squares of rubber which I cut from the prophylactics readily obtainable at the Guardroom. My battledress pockets were full of these condoms, cut into squares, or nestling in their little packets.

Bump! I hit the ground. A perfect Summer's day in France, except that Germans were advancing on all sides, armed with guns, sticks, hammers, pick-axes. Their leader was young, blond, a perfect Aryan, pistol in his hand.

"Pick up your parachute and follow me!" he said. "Pick it up yourself," I said, experiencing a sudden rush of adrenalin. He shouted an order in German. His subordinate came to attention and stretched out his right arm (I had believed it only happened in Pinewood films).

"Heil Hitler!" he cried. I giggled. It was a mistake. Someone frog-marched me to a small hut. We all crowded inside. I felt very vulnerable. The adrenalin had melted away. The officer began his search. He took my watch, took a few pounds in money and arrived at my battledress top. My secret hoard was thrown on the table. A dozen French letters, some mutilated, some in their packets, some loose. He picked up one by its little rubber end, regarded it in the sunlight. He smiled.

"You vill not be needing zeese!" he said.

John Cruickshank VC

Contemplating on remembrance I recall the words of Our Lord Jesus Christ to His disciples on the occasion of the Last Supper, "This do in remembrance of me." These words are part of the Christian ceremony of Holy Communion where participants are reminded of His life, teachings and His supreme sacrifice for humanity.

The word 'Remembrance' is significant and likewise is used to describe the services and occasions where we gather to honour our war dead. These solemn occasions allow us to reflect reverently on their lives and their supreme sacrifice for our civilisation.

Sir Marcus Worsley Bart

If an individual loses his memory, his capacity to cope with life is drastically limited. The same is true of a nation. We should not live in the past (as some nations do), but we ought to live remembering the past and therefore learning from it.

Particularly is this true about remembering those who have died for their country in the past. We are grateful for their sacrifice, from which we benefit, but above all we need to remember the lessons they learnt so tragically.

Above all we must never forget as was first said some two hundred years ago: "The condition upon which God has given liberty to man is eternal vigilance." That lesson is as relevant today as it ever was.

Norris McWhirter CBE

Being born in 1925, my late twin brother Ross and I were able to volunteer in Salisbury for wartime service in the Royal Navy. We were, aged 18, duly commissioned Midshipmen RNVR on the same day in 1944. Our school at Marlborough lost over 1,000 lives in the two World Wars. Our Roll of Honour contains the names of 15 VCs and GCs of whom seven were posthumous.

All this sacrifice was in the name of liberty, justice, allegiance and in the defence of the sovereignty of our island nation. It has been heartbreaking to see our allegiance to the Queen supplanted and to witness our self-governance ended on 1st November 1993. The next generation will ere long redress the actions of some of the present generation, provided they nurture the spirit of remembrance for those generations, without whose sacrifice we would not be here.

Harry Carpenter

I joined the Royal Navy in 1943 at the age of 17 and worked, both at home and abroad, as what was then called a wireless telegraphist, tapping away in Morse code.

Early in 1944 I was drafted to the Mediterranean area and at the time of the D-Day landings was plying between Malta and Sicily on the destroyer, HMS *Whaddon*.

The following year, when the war in Europe ended, I was on board another ship, making my way back to England.

So, my view of those historic events was from afar and I was spared what so many others went through in order to rid Europe of its appalling subjugation.

But I can still vividly remember the relief that swept over me, as we steamed closer to home, that it was all over, at least in Europe.

It is not easy today to make younger people understand that in the earlier days of the war, there seemed to be nothing but struggle and suffering ahead, perhaps for 10 years or longer. It was a long time before light appeared at the end of the tunnel.

As fate decreed, I had it easy in my Navy years, but still

today I owe an enormous debt of gratitude to those who paid for my freedom with their lives.

Bryan Cowgill

Tom Crabtree bowled a peach of an outswinger and you did well to get your bat out of its way. He was a talented and graceful young cricketer much admired by his contemporaries, not to mention those like me who were his junior by a couple of years or so and whose admiration contained more than a tinge of hero worship.

Tom died in 1943 at the age of nineteen, killed in a bombing run on his first mission with the crew of an RAF Lancaster.

I still think of him more than half a century later and not just in the silence at our home town Cenotaph on Remembrance Day.

It's not as if he was a relative or even a classmate because of the difference in the number of our tender years. But Tom has always figured in ones memories of those far-off summer days when we played together on the cricket fields of our youth – and my mind keeps a frozen frame of that shocking day when we heard he was missing, believed killed in action.

My own two sons have heard from me about my friend Tom Crabtree and know about him even though they were born thirty years after he lived.

No one truly dies while there is someone to remember him and pass on his memory. That's what I believe.

Bryan Cowgill who was Head of BBC Television Sport between 1963-1973, and Controller of BBC1 between 1973-1977, is pictured here in 1944 while serving as a 2nd Lieutenant 40 Royal Marine Commando.
(Photo courtesy Bryan Cowgill)

Field Marshal Sir Roland Gibbs
GCB CBE DSO MC

I saw the war in the Western Desert, in Italy and in North-West Europe. I saw the losses in young men, ours and the enemy's, in battles such as Alamein, the Normandy bridgehead, the Falaise Gap and in many smaller battles in which my soldiers were involved and where each casualty was a personal loss. War is hateful and wasteful. But we had to go to war, because there seemed to be no end to the evils of Nazi Germany.

Since then we have been involved in many small wars, and no doubt more will happen. But a future major war is likely to be destructive beyond imagination. I would hope that by remembering the last war we will remind ourselves of this: and that the best way to prevent such a catastrophy is to keep our most successful alliance, NATO, strong and active.

Field Marshal The Lord Bramall
KG GCB OBE MC JP

I was fifteen when the Second World War started and had, only a few years previously, visited Germany on holiday where I had seen for myself some outward signs (for instance in the public campaign against the Jews) of the cruel and callous oppression which were to be the hallmarks of Nazi tyranny. Then the rest of my school days were punctuated by the imminent threat of invasion, the Battle of Britain and the Blitz on the London area – exciting perhaps for someone in their teens, but traumatic enough for many.

At any rate when, on leaving school and like so many others of my age joining the Forces, I was to experience the realities of battle at first hand, I had no doubt that if ever a war was a just one, this was it. For we were manifestly up against one of the most evil and devilish regimes the world had ever seen, in which the sort of things which have since been happening in Bosnia and Croatia were commonplace and even institutionalised, and it had to be overcome if civilisation was to survive.

Nor must we ever forget that it was only by the skin of our teeth that we were able to survive the first three years of the war and ultimately get the right answer; and had it not been for the collective efforts and, in many cases, sacrifice of so many people, we would not have been able to keep the way open for civilised society. The world would have been an altogether more barren and brutal place for all of us and particularly for our children and grandchildren to grow up in.

We therefore have a continuing obligation to remember and to say thank you to those who sacrificed so much for our victory, for truly, as that lovely inscription on the war memorial at Kohima reminds us: 'For our tomorrow, they (those who went to war and did not come back) gave their today'.

Lord Hanson

Life seems to be full of anniversaries of one sort or another. Ably assisted by the media, we are constantly urged to look into the past. We are encouraged to remember, as we do now for example the heroic events of fifty years ago when the last . . . . and we must hope it was the last . . . . World War came to an end. But I believe that the true value of remembering, the real contribution that the Royal British Legion brings to us today, even for those for whom anything over a few years ago is ancient history, is to the welfare and wellbeing of present and future generations. The past is another country.

It is the good work the Legion has done and does today that matters. Looking after the living is its true worth, for while conflicts exist there will always be casualties to be helped adjust to their new lives. Of course people need to be reminded of the evils and heroisms of the past. This is not for sentimental reasons but so that that past is not allowed to repeat itself in the years ahead. Long may the Royal British Legion hold the banner of present and future caring and concern for our less fortunate fellow men and women.

Sir John Harvey-Jones MBE

Before the last war I was in training as a professional naval officer which meant that I became involved in the war from a very early age. During that time I lost a number of my colleagues and friends at sea.

The experiences of war and, more particularly, my experiences after the war, of serving in a completely collapsed Germany led to my strong belief in the necessity for a united Europe. Young people of the age at which I formed these views and had these experiences have, fortunately, been spared the harsh lessons which I and my generation were forced to learn. It is, therefore, all the more important that those of us who survived should do our best to try and ensure that the lessons of the war are not forgotten, and that young people bear these matters in mind when forming their own views of the future of our continent.

St. Austell Bay, Bermuda, October 1954. Sir John Harvey-Jones (front row, second from left) had served throughout the Second World War in the Royal Navy.
(Photo courtesy Sir John Harvey-Jones)

Lord Barber of Wentbridge

I am one of the lucky ones who came through the War unscathed. As Chairman of the Royal Air Force Benevolent Fund I come across many sad cases where we are able to help. 50 years is a long time ago, but we must never forget those who suffered to keep our country free.

Lord Aberconway

To forget those who risked, and lost, their lives for this country, in two great wars, is the height of ingratitude.

Yet as the years pass, there are fewer of us left who participated in those fearsome days and who thus can recall vividly the sense of loss and admiration at the sight of colleagues being killed, and news of friends suffering that fate. It is therefore all the more important that those too young to have such vivid memories, and have to rely on written or imagined awareness of the events of fifty or more years ago, should still be encouraged to recognise and pay tribute to those who saved this country in those dark, dire days. They came from all over the world. Our debt to them is immeseaurable, and must not be allowed to fade from our thoughts.

Lord Graham of Edmonton

Having served in the Royal Marines during the Second World War, I do not need to be reminded of the sacrifices which were made by many men and women in order that the War was won and peace achieved. Personally, I find it incredible that these times between 1939 and 1945 now deserve a 50th Anniversary. It provides us with the opportunity of paying full tribute to those who gave their lives and those who suffered. The latter includes many people who never saw battle but who lost loved ones. The price of freedom is eternal vigilance and that is why I am happy in this very small way to associate myself with this venture.

General Sir John Hackett MC

The moral obligation not to forget the human sacrifice and the huge destruction a general war brings on mankind cannot be over-stated. There are other reasons for remembrance. Given the appalling destructive power of war-fighting technology and of weapon systems developed since the end of the Second World War, it is blindingly obvious to anyone that there must never be another one. A purely moral argument, strong though it is, finds powerful support from allied victory in the last world war, followed in due course by the collapse of a world-wide threat from totalitarian communism. We have been given a breathing space, but no thinking person can suppose we are now finally out of danger of world war. We are surrounded today by conflict in a highly unstable and heavily armed world. If we forget what survival in the Second World War has cost mankind, and refuse to see the manifest danger in the world today that there could easily be a third, we do so at our peril. It is not, therefore, sentimentality alone which causes regret at a diminished recognition of the dangers survived and the very high cost in human suffering of our survival. It is also a simple matter of insurance. We dare not forget what survival has already cost mankind as we move on into a no less dangerous future. To continue to remember, and to maintain a high level of remembrance while making sure that succeeding generations understand and recognise its importance, is a matter of self-interest no less than of duty. There can be no question of our failing to meet what on so many counts is an urgent obligation. Those of us who went through it all last time can find no excuse for a failure to remember. It is succeeding generations who have to recognise the danger to us all, and the part to be played in its avoidance in the future by remembrance of what happened in the past.

Facing page: General Sir John Hackett was wounded at Arnhem in 1944, while in command of Four Parachute Brigade. He was also wounded in Syria In 1941, and the Western Desert in 1942, winning the MC and DSO and bar.
(Photo courtesy General Sir John Hackett).

Professor Lord Beloff FBA.

Memories fade and the task of understanding how those of a previous generation felt is not an easy one for the young. It is therefore worth while recalling for their benefit the extent to which the world they inherited was made possible only by the sacrifice of those who fought off the greatest threat that Britain had ever faced. None of the countries that suffered from the Nazi conquest and occupation has altogether recovered from the experience; that we did not undergo that experience should be an argument in favour of dedicating ourselves to preserving those aspects of British life we most wish to hand on.

My own wartime experiences unlike that of most of my friends was a curiously detached one. My military service in the invasion winter of 1940–1941 was brief and never took me further afield than the coast of North Wales. Having been invalided out after less than a year, it was through the experience of others that one learned about the war and the horrors that it revealed. And often one's contempories were so keen to get on with their interrupted lives that they were reticent about their experiences, one only very gradually learned about what they had achieved.

Some, one never saw again – those that we remember. What their sacrifice should have brought home to succeeding generations was that dangers do not go away when they are ignored. The pacifism of the inter-war decades in which I shared, helped to convince the dictators that they could act with impunity. I have been saddened to see in the younger generation – sometimes encouraged by those who should have known better – some of the same attitudes cropping up again. To recall what happened the last time, cannot be but a good idea.

Max Bygraves

People who remember say, "Let's hope there'll never be another one." The only way to make sure that there isn't another one, is to remember!

Max Bygraves.

CHAPTER THREE

CHILDREN AT WAR

Some of our strongest recollections come from our childhood, this being especially true for the children who lived through the war experience, and whose memories are enhanced by a disjointed and quite extraordinary succession of events, which burned lasting imagery into their minds. Their experiences are so far removed from the normality of our own childhoods, that it is difficult to know exactly how they felt or what lasting effects these events were to have. The ironic thing is of course, that for babies born just prior to the war, or during its early stages, horror and sorrow were very much a normality of life, for they knew no difference.

For many children it must have been like a larger than life adventure, or an extension to their play and games, drawing an uneasy line between imagination and reality. Others had their childhood abruptly shortened by the advent of personal suffering or family sorrow, against a backdrop of horrific proportions.

At the very onset of the war an evacuation scheme was set into motion, the idea of which was to move huge numbers of children from areas which were considered to be in danger of Nazi air attack, or land battle in the event of an invasion. These children were moved in huge numbers to safer areas such as the West Country, Wales or Northumberland. Quite often children were unaccompanied, others moved with their mothers. There was also a provision in the scheme to relocate, sometimes temporarily, expectant mothers. This provision also facilitated them with necessary medical treatment and professional care.

The main areas for concern would naturally have been our major cities. London in particular, saw the mass Exodus of entire schools. Thousands of unaccompanied children moved by train to new, and uncertain futures. For many these must have been traumatic times. For others, yet another chance to interchange between the reality of life and the adventure of imagination.

Children who had been evacuated from the excitement of the city, especially during these extraordinary times, must have felt suddenly isolated from the events which were taking place. It would be naive to suggest that they were too young to have taken an interest in the progress of the war. After all, many of them had fathers, brothers or uncles, who were serving in the armed forces, and mothers who were still living in areas subjected to intense bombing. Mothers may have been confident about the safety of their children, but the children themselves would have been very worried about the rest of their families. The terrible upheaval and emotional stress to even the youngest child, is another consequence of modern war, which must never be forgotten.

As well as an understanding of sorrow and sacrifice, either at personal or international level, children from that time were undoubtedly insenced by the tremendous community spirit. They must have felt very proud of the nation and her people. Another thing which we perhaps fail to appreciate now, is that when these youngsters saw their fathers going off to war – then their older brothers when their time came – they naturally assumed that one day they would also have to go and fight. The war was everything and everywhere, dictating almost everything that people did and how they thought. Children would have taken this for granted, unsuspecting that one day there would be peace and their fathers would stay at home and go to work in factories and offices. The generation of war children grew up firmly expecting to be recalled to arms and quite prepared to carry on the cause. Now, as new generations have evolved through progressively peaceful times, we atlast have young people who don't live in the fear of being expected to lay down their lives during future conflicts.

Those who were children during the Second World War, perhaps appreciate more than any of us, the sacrifices that were made, and the gaps that were left in their communities. This understanding and appreciation had been a driving force in many, to uphold the tradition of Remembrance and endeavour to pass its spirit down through the generations.

In Britain, Victory in Europe Day, must have been one of the greatest occasions the country had ever seen. The nation sighed with such relief that children would have been aware that this was much more than just a street party of epic proportion. Little did they know, or could even guess, that the peace which their fathers created was going to last for 50 years. Peace is one of the most important messages in our act of Remembrance because the Hero generation paid for our peace with everything they had, body and soul.

Lord (Jeffrey) Archer of Weston-super-Mare

I was born in 1940 and spent the first eighteen years of my life in Mark and Weston-super-Mare in Somerset. I vividly remember soldiers returning home crippled and blind and some who did not return. I took for granted it was just part of normal life.

Now when I see Weston-super-Mare with its bright lights, young people and no bombed out buildings I am thankful this country has not been at war for nearly fifty years. I am among those who hopes the next generation will remember Kipling's words . . . . 'Lest we forget – lest we forget!'

Paul Flynn MP

Empty desks at St. Patricks' school in Grangetown meant more families had been wiped out in the previous night's blitz. Here was eloquent testimony to the waste, cruelty and futility of war.

Lord Arran

Towards the end of the war, when as a child, aged 5 or 6 and living in Hertfordshire, my mother flung me to the ground and threw herself on top of me. A 'V' bomb was passing above, the engine had cut out and we prayed that it would not land on us. It didn't, it landed in a field not far away a few seconds later. After a short time we went to look at the hole it had made. It was enormous. I remember thinking what would happen if it had landed on a town; and, of course, so many did, and so many were killed.

Richard Briers

I remember my father and I watching the Spitfires pass over us on their way to battle and counting the few that returned home. How saddened we were at the news of the sinking of the great battleship the *Hood* with all those young men who gave their lives to save ours. The debt is unpayable. We must never forget that.

I remember my father and I watching the Spitfires pass over us on their way to battle and counting the few that returned home. How saddened we were at the news of the sinking of the great battleship 'THE HOOD' with all those young men who gave their lives to save ours. The debt is unpayable. We must never forget that

RICHARD BRIERS

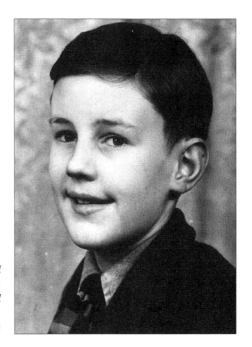

Comic actor Richard Briers would watch the Spitfires with his father, on their way to do battle, saddened by the few which returned. (Photo courtesy Richard Briers)

John Smith MP

My most compelling involvement in remembrance of the Second World War was when I visited the small Dutch village of Ter Apel on the Dutch/German border to visit the grave of my uncle, Flying Officer Peter Scott, RAFVR, who was a pilot in the RAF Pathfinder Force and who was killed when his plane was shot down over Ter Apel in 1943. The crew, mostly Canadian, were buried beside him in the beautifully cared for graveyard. The local people, who remembered the night when the plane was shot down, were able to recollect the occasion vividly. At some risk to themselves they had secured a proper burial for the crew. I took photographs for my mother, who is Peter's older sister, and for his other brothers and sister.

When my uncle was home on leave not long before he was killed in action I had proudly walked up the village street with the handsome young officer with the wings on his uniform.

Most of us have such direct connections with the heroism and sacrifice of those who died that we might be free. We must never forget their sacrifice or cease to honour their heroism.

Lord Tebbit

I remember listening as a boy of eight to Mr Chamberlain's broadcast telling us that we were at war with Germany.

My father had survived four years of army service in the 1914–18 war. Although he never spoke of it I knew war was a terrible and overpowering thing so I dashed to the window to see what had happened, how things had changed. To my amazement nothing had changed and life seemed as normal as it had the day before.

Before long the sirens sounded in the first of many air raid alerts though a false one on this occasion.

I grew up in a world in which bombs, V1s and V2s were part of everyday life, accepting that like my father and uncles I would sooner or later go to war myself.

National service, when it came, seemed a preparation for that day.

Now my children, who grew up under the shadow of the threat of nuclear war but without ever carrying arms, are raising children who we hope will be free from the threat of war.

Perhaps there is now a danger that the threat is no longer recognised and as we who remember the reality of war die out, then the danger will return.

So let 1995 mark not just fifty years without a major European war, but let it be a year to renew the resolve to make the sacrifices needed to ensure peace.

Leslie Thomas

During the First World War my father served in the Royal Artillery in France. Gunner Thomas told many a tale of his adventures, some of them hilarious (as when he sold a horse to a French farmer). But his photograph from that time shows him with two 'wound stripes' on his uniform sleeve.

At the age of fifty ("I'm the same age as Hitler" he used to say) he was at war again, this time as a Merchant Seaman. When he could have been ashore in the Home Guard or as an Air Raid Warden, he was stoking the boilers of a ship on the dangerous ocean. He went on one of the Arctic convoys to Russia and came home very solemn, telling of torpedoed ships blowing up in the icy seas. My brother and I were at school and we were thrilled by his stories. Only he knew how close to danger he was. March, 1943 was the worst month for Merchant shipping losses of the war. Had not the new detector devices of the Allies come into use then it is doubtful whether the war would have taken the course it did. In the middle of that month, in our council house in Newport, South Wales, we received a letter from him posted in Sierra Leone. He very rarely wrote and my brother and I were still arguing over who would have the foreign stamps when the news came that he was 'missing presumed lost'. He was aboard the cargo ship S.S. *Empire Whale* which was torpedoed in the Atlantic with the loss of more than fifty lives.

The name of David James Thomas is on the Merchant Navy Memorial at Tower Hill in London. I have taken my children to see it. They were astonished at all the thousands of names there, alongside that of the grandfather they never knew. I try to impress them that it is because of Jim Thomas and men like him that they are able to live as they do today.

Dame Jill Knight DBE MP

To many of us who have personal memories of the 1939–45 War, the realisation that it ended fifty years ago is incredible. In some ways the memories of those days are sharper and clearer than things that happened a mere ten years ago. I well recall, as a schoolgirl, trying to do my homework under the dining room table with the 'crump' of the occasional bomb falling quite audible. My family followed the general rule of the time that, when a raid started, the safest place was either in the cupboard under the stairs or under any available table. Luckily our house was never hit although Birmingham and the industrial heart of Britain were certainly a target. I shall never forget the bombing of Coventry, not very far away from where we lived. I served as a WAAF later myself, and was in Germany at the end of the war.

With the passage of time, inevitably many many people today have no such recollections but our country must never forget the sacrifices made to win the war against Hitler and, over and above everything else, the sacrifice made by so many brave men and women at that time.

Peter Bowles

My mum and dad often took me up to Huntingdon to see Grannie and Grandad (my father's parents).

They lived in a row of cottages which were gas lit downstairs and candle lit above. My father had tried to persuade them to have electricity and a wireless but they were rather nervous of them (my grandfather was born in 1864).

Every evening the ritual was that my grandad having come back from his allotment would have a cup of tea, then wash and shave in the back scullery. Then he would go upstairs and appear in his suit with stiff collar and tie. All this was so he could respectably present himself next door, where they had a wireless. It was nearly time for the six o'clock news. Grandad would reappear at 6.32 or so, and mum and grannie and me would sit around Grandad in his small bed room while he stood and retold us the News from the BBC. This was done every evening without fail and was a very important ritual during the war. Of course, when we were not there his only audience would have been Grandma.

Even as a young child I was in no doubt that something important was happening and, everyone in the land was involved in beating the enemy.

A child at war. The most vivid memories of actor Peter Bowles relate to his regular visits to see his grandparents in Huntingdon. Every evening at six o'clock, his grandfather would put on his suit with stiff collar and tie and present himself next door – where they had a wireless set. (Photo courtesy Peter Bowles)

Television personality Michael Aspel (left) in 1941/2, aged 8/9. The photograph was taken during his evacuation to Chard in Somerset. (Photo courtesy Bagenal Harvey Organisation).

Michael Aspel OBE

I remember sitting by the wireless set with the rest of my family, listening to Neville Chamberlain announcing that we were at war with Germany. I was six years old at the time, and was terrified that it meant that the Nazis would be marching down our street before the day was out.

A few months later my mother was left alone in our small London flat. My father had joined the army, and my sister and brother and I were evacuees. I was separated from them and spent the next four and a half years virtually as an only child. Visits from our parents were rare. The greatest excitement was when American troops were stationed nearby, prior to D-Day. We all ran errands for them and became their mascots. It was a sad morning when we discovered a deserted camp with a few scrawled farewell messages and souvenirs left behind. Many of our heroes would have been killed soon afterwards.

I finally came home just before the end of the war and was horrified to see the devastation – shells of buildings, whole streets missing.

No young person should have to experience the ripples of pain caused by war, and no young person should be unaware of what was done by ordinary people who wanted nothing more than to be happily at home, but responded to the call with courage and without hesitation.

Bill Gunston

When the Second World War ended I was 18. At that time I had gained a Higher Schools Certificate (the 1944 exam was taken with a watcher on the roof who pressed a button if a 'V-1' Flying Bomb looked certain to blow out the school windows). In my spare time I had also been Librarian of the London Philharmonic and a flight-test observer with de Havilland Aircraft on Mosquito production. I had also become Flight Sergeant in my school Air Training Corps squadron, flying on every possible opportunity (there were many) and was on deferred service from pilot training with the RAF.

But I had never even kissed a girl (sex figured in childish jokes, but it never occurred to me or any of my friends that we could actually practise it). I had never smoked, never been drunk, never vandalised anything, never stolen anything and regarded the police as an undermanned force (because of the war) whom we helped in many ways. We simply didn't realise how deprived we were. As a result we were happy as the day is long. Psychiatric help – well, we could spell it correctly, but had never heard of anyone needing it.

I cannot imagine anything worse than being bored. Truly 'the devil finds work for idle hands', and I feel desperately sorry for today's mixed-up kids who steal and burn cars or anything else that takes their fancy. Is it really fun to put on the colours of a football club simply in order to indulge in gang warfare? Are we really rushing faster than the Romans did towards total debauchery and economic downfall?

Many young people today may think of the Second World War as a time of misery and terror. So it was, for those under Hitler's rule. But for a young man in beleaguered Britain it was a time strangely free from any problem except that there was never enough time. On an average day I probably cycled 15 miles, and it seemed that every mile was into rain and a headwind. But we all did our best. We all pulled together. Nobody thought of doing anything else.

In 1966 an American scientist, Herman Khan, said to me "Your country is going to the dogs. What you need is 200 million hostile Arabs screaming round your shores." Well, we've done our best to destroy our own manufacturing industries and alienate everyone else – not just the Arabs – so with a bit of luck we might eventually become impoverished, deprived and socially responsible, like we were in the War.

Betty Boothroyd

When the very first sirens sounded I was told by my parents to shelter under the kitchen table. In later raids we all made for my school's air-raid shelter. I was never bombed but the possibility of being bombed was always present in the minds of wartime children.

I remember particularly my mother always taking a biscuit tin to the shelter. It contained family documents such as birth certificates and the all-important insurance policies. She reckoned that a biscuit tin would keep them safe through fire.

I was very proud of my siren suit. It was made from a blanket and dyed purple. To me it seemed just like Winston Churchill's more famous siren suit. I wore it over my pyjamas whenever we went to the shelter.

I started growing up to the sound of the ack-ack guns stationed on a cliff above my home town of Dewsbury and the accompanying wail of the air-raid sirens. I used to hope that we would not get the all-clear until 2 a.m. If it came after 2 a.m. we did not have to go to school the next morning.

But most of all I remember the elder brothers of my friends coming home on leave. We always said "How nice to see you." And then, inevitably, we asked "When are you going back?"

For we knew they had to go back to their units all too soon. And some of them never returned to us. To the end of my life I shall remember what we still owe to them.

Chris Bonington CBE

Iwas born in 1934 and so can just remember the Second World War. My school in Kent was evacuated to the north of England when the threat of invasion arose after the collapse of France. I can also remember air raids when I was at home in Hampstead and seeing the con trails of fighters and bombers as they set out on their missions.

I am intensely aware of how much all of us owe to the soldiers, sailors and airmen who fought for our liberty and the democratic value that we hold dear. It was their courage that saved the British Isles from being invaded in 1940. Had Britain fallen the history of the world could have been very different. Not only we, but the entire world owes a great deal to those men and women who fought for us in the Second World War.

Chris Bonington CBE

31st January, 1994

I was born in 1934 and so can just remember the Second World War. My school in Kent was evacuated to the north of England when the threat of invasion arose after the collapse of France. I can also remember air raids when I was at home in Hampstead and seeing the con trails of fighters and bombers as they set out on their missions. I am intensely aware of how much all of us owe to the soldiers, sailors and airmen who fought for our liberty and the democratic values that we hold dear. It was their courage that saved the British Isles from being invaded in 1940. Had Britain fallen the history of the world could have been very different. Not only we, but the entire world owes a great deal to those men and women who fought for us in the Second World War.

Chris Bonington

Robin Knox-Johnston CBE

The whole of my early life was dominated by the war. Father, something of a stranger and making only occasional appearances in uniform. Rationing, blackouts, the sounds of bombers, the crump of bombs, being carried into air raid shelters, soldiers, tanks, Americans in huge trucks chewing gum and if you were lucky, throwing you a piece. These were the memories as one struggled with the more normal demands of starting school and growing up in a temporary single parent family. It was the same for all my generation only my brothers and I were lucky. Unlike many we mixed with at school, our father did eventually achieve something called being de-mobbed and came home two years after the Japanese surrender, by which time I was eight years old and had to come to terms with this stranger who now dictated my family life.

Loss was almost a normal occurance. We grew up hardened to it, at such a young age we assumed it was the normal way of life, it was impossible to imagine what peace meant except we would be able to buy unlimited sweets. Everyone knew someone who had lost a father, a son, brother or uncle, and as the attacks on the homeland developed, mothers, sisters, aunts and daughters were added to the list. The appalling total was nearly half a million people in Britain alone.

Despite thirty years as a reservist I have never heard a shot fired in anger. I owe that to the sacrifice of those who fell in the war.

Lord Wakeham

My memories of the war are fleeting and necessarily highly personal for a small boy of six.

My first was of my father getting a telegram whilst we were on the beach in August 1939 instructing him to rejoin his TA Unit.

I also clearly remember the declaration of war on 3 September 1939 and for the rest it is a mixture of strange houses and boarding school until VE Day in 1945 by which time I was back home in the house from which I heard the

12245678910111213141516171819202122232425

declaration of war.

During the intervening years for one reason or another I lived in Surrey, East Anglia, Northumberland, North Wales, Westmorland, Scotland, Hertfordshire, Worcestershire, Berkshire, Gloucestershire, Buckinghamshire and I think Hampshire. As far as I can remember I lived in over 25 different houses.

I remember also many long train journeys with the trains full with servicemen, British, GIs and Canadians, who always seemed to have sweets available for us children.

It only slowly dawned on me the full significance of the events and the sacrifices made by so many that the world may be free. All of us have cause to be grateful.

Lord Parkinson

I was only eight when War was declared in 1939 and I still remember Neville Chamberlain's broadcast to the nation very clearly. I remember the despair I felt after Dunkirk and the thrilling success of the Battle of Britain, but the most exciting moment of all was the end of the Second World War in Europe. I lived in the North of England at the time, in my home town of Carnforth, and I remember a marvellous series of street parties when whole neighbourhoods celebrated together.

My generation was too young to fight in the war, but was deeply affected by it and many of us became involved in politics as a result. We were determined to try to play a part in ensuring that a third World War never came about.

Richard Alexander MP

I was 10 when the war ended and was evacuated to Aberdeenshire for most of the war, so my memories of war as such are very dim. Yet we were made conscious at school, and by my mother at home, that far away there were men and women fighting against an evil power, often never to return. In turn when my time came I spent two years in the Army doing National Service during the most serious part of the Cold War and although I never fired a rifle in anger, I was aware of being part of a British tradition of being willing to defend our country in time of need.

I am now a member of the Fellowship of the Services in my constituency and most of my companions there are World War II men whose courage and dedication when their country needed them were never in doubt. I don't think I have missed more than one Remembrance Sunday in the past 30 years and hope to go on remembering those who did give their lives as long as life is left in me.

Lord Mackay of Clashfern

I was a boy at school during the war. I saw the enthusiasm of the soldiers anxious to repel the advance of cruel aggression. I remember most clearly the anxiety we all felt over their safe return and the deep grief and sense of loss we experienced when a familiar face failed to come home. Those deep emotions have added to my own personal determination that their contribution to the safety and welfare of us all should not be taken for granted. Whenever we are discouraged, we should remember the enormous sacrifice they made and ensure that they are never forgotten.

Lord Howe of Aberavon

The conflicts of the Second World War coincided almost exactly with my time at Winchester. The College provided a haven of peace and reason for those of us who were lucky enough to be there. There was some terrible turbulence, certianly: air raids; Home Guard duties; fire-watching and food rationing; regular briefings from General Montgomery (his son, David, was in the school); but we were spared the real horrors of war.

Even so, it was impossible for anyone in my generation at Winchester to forget Britain's European vocation or our commitment to the cause of freedom. The conflict taking place, sometimes literally above our heads, was adding its own toll to the Roll of Honour – from Crimea to Cambrai,

Geoffrey Howe in 1940/41, his first year at Winchester. The College provided a haven of peace and reason for those who were lucky enough to be there during such troubled times. (Photo courtesy The Lord Howe of Aberavon).

past which we walked to class each day.

The last Wkyehamist to serve as Foreign Secretary, Lord Grey of Fallodon, described how, in 1914, he saw the lights going out all over Europe. It was my privilege to serve in the same office at a time when the lights of freedom were coming on again throughout Europe, East as well as West.

But already 'the brutal and destructive side of modern nationalism', as Isaiah Berlin has called it, was revealing itself with unattractive force. And once again people are being killed in conflicts upon our continent.

We must remember afresh the reasons why so many Europeans have died in war in centuries past. Never again should Europe be engulfed by such futile internecine strife. We must renew our commitment to the cause of reconciliation and peace.

David Shepherd OBE

At the time of the Battle of Britain in the summer of 1940, I was one of those typical 'spotty' little school boys, aged 9, with a cloth cap and short pant, featured in so many photographs of the time. I was indeed evacuated to Scotland for 3 weeks but I soon came back again like so many other evacuees, to my home in North London. We had all our windows blown out by the Germans and, with my brother, we used to collect war souvenirs from incendiary bombs in the field next door, and bits and pieces from crashed German aeroplanes. Going to the school on the bus we used to watch the aerial fighting overhead between the Hurricanes and the Messerschmitts and life was one huge excitement.

I remember my brother and I raising 60 pounds – quite a lot of money in those days for 'Spitfire Week'. I remember also queuing up with a lot of other grubby boys to spend our allotted couple of minutes in the cockpits of reasonably undamaged German Aircraft which were displayed in the village square, to raise money. We did more damage to that German aeroplane than the RAF did shooting it down, pinching every piece that was moveable before the next boy in the queue did so. I still have those souvenirs, treasured memories of exciting days for a small boy.

We had no idea in our immature minds that people were killing each other as we watched the aerial battles overhead and experienced these amazing days at first hand. Perhaps it was just a few years later that the realisation of the horror of it all came to me. I went to Stowe Public School, situated in the peace and tranquility of the remote Buckinghamshire countryside. I remember so vividly reading the headlines in the newspapers when the bestiality of the concentration camps was brought to the attention of the world. This was happening just a couple of hundred miles away from where we, school boys, were living, relatively, on the 'fat of the land.' We were not responsible but we could not help feeling the sense of shame and may it never happen again.

Claire Rayner

I was a child of the Blitz. At the age of 9 I spent 28 hours under seven feet of rubble and that was an experience that has left me with a hatred of war and everything to do with it. I am torn in half by remembrance; I know it is essential that people remember bad events so that they don't allow them to happen again – as a philosopher said, those who forget history are condemned for ever to repeat it. But sadly some remembrance turns into a form of glorification of war and I hate that kind. I loathe seeing soldiers marching to the beat of drums as a way of reminding us there have been bloody, horrible and death dealing wars in the past; memories should be full of regret and not of glory.

Sir John Cope MP

When I was young, during and after the Second World War, I stood beside my father on Remembrance Day and shared a little of his memories of being on the Somme and at Ypres in the First World War. Since he died I think back on that and treasure the fading photographs of those he went to France with, so many of whom did not return.

Much more recently, as a Northern Ireland Minister, I have stood in remembrance beside those who have lost loved ones in recent years to terrorist bombs and guns.

It is right to recall those from every conflict who have risked and lost their lives, their health and happiness, to preserve our freedoms and the rule of justice and law.

Tom Stoppard

I was eight when the war ended, and have never been called upon to put on a uniform. I often reflect on my good fortune, and on those who were not so fortunate. I have four sons who have never had to fight a war, and, God willing, never will. Over the years I have read dozens of war memoirs from 1939–45. I still read them occassionally and nowadays I am chastened by knowing that I am often reading about people younger than my sons, people who carried out extraordinary exploits and showed great courage, and sometimes died. What is chastening is the sense of having escaped scot free, as a citizen and as a parent. Remembering those who did not escape is the very least we owe. It is a privilege to contribute to the Royal British Legion's Book of Remembrance.

"I was eight when the war ended, and have never been called upon to put on a uniform. I often reflect on my good fortune, and on those who were not so fortunate. I have four sons who have never had to fight a war and, God Willing, never will. Over the years I have read dozens of war memoirs from 1939-45. I still read them occasionally and nowadays I am chastened by knowing that I am often reading about people younger than my sons, people who carried out extraordinary exploits and showed great courage, and sometimes died. What is chastening is the sense of having escaped scot free, as a citizen and as a parent. Remembering those who did not escape is the very least we owe. It is a privilege to contribute to the Royal British Legion's Book of Remembrance."

Yours sincerely,

Tom Stoppard

*Member of today's Parliament,
Tim Sainsbury at his
childhood studies while Britain
waged war.
(Photo courtesy
Tim Sainsbury)*

Tim Sainsbury MP

During the first week of the war, as a seven year old, I remember my late grandmother saying in the air raid shelter to which we had gone when the sirens went, "If it goes on like this, it won't last six weeks."

No bombs fell then – I think it was a false alarm. Little did we know how long it would last or how many would lose their lives or be injured in the conflict. That is why we should remember.

Sir Keith Speed RD MP

Fifty years on from the end of the Second World War, we do well to remember the efforts and sacrifices of millions of our fellow citizens in the United Kingdom Armed Forces who with our Allies combined to defeat the evils of Nazi Germany and Imperial Japan.

I spent my formative years as a child during the Second World War and my father and many of my family served in the Armed Forces and indeed an Uncle was taken prisoner of war at Arnhem.

It is very important that the Royal British Legion reminds present and future generations of the sacrifices made by their forebears and of the hard truth that the price of liberty is eternal vigilance.

Marshal of the Royal Air Force
Sir Keith Williamson CGB AFC RAF

I was born in 1928 and so I grew up very much in the shadow of a World War that had shattered the lives of my parents' generation. My own family had been very directly affected by that war. My mother's only brother was killed in 1915 by the same German shell that seriously injured my father. My father's only brother was also badly injured at about the same time while serving in the same regiment.

I did not know all this in my earliest years, but I was nevertheless aware of an almost tangible sense of sadness and melancholy that intruded on all our family gatherings as I grew up. Indeed, my grandmother, who lived until she was over ninety years old, never ceased to grieve for the loss of her only son.

It was only in his later years that my father could bring himself to talk about the time that he spent in the trenches, and by then we had emerged from yet another war in which he had seen our family home destroyed by a German V2 weapon. Looking back on that time it seems inconceivable that the terrible lessons of the First World War could have been so quickly forgotten and that Europe could have allowed itself to be engulfed yet again.

This must never be allowed to happen again. We have now been at peace for almost fifty years, but if that peace is to be truly lasting I believe that it is very important that future generations are regularly reminded of the terrible cost in human terms of the alternative.

Peter Temple-Morris MP

I well remember the Second World War although I was far too young to fight in it but somehow grew up with the thought that one day I might have to, like so many others before me, fight for the freedoms that now seem to be presumed as a natural right. Because I never had to I have read many books on the subject and am very well aware of the sacrifices that so many people made when the call came. I can do no more than sincerely and with some knowledge salute them!

The importance of remembrance is quite simply that in this world we should never assume anything as of right. The act of remembrance and acknowledgement of sacrifice is something that is very important for the future.

Graham Bright MP

I was born during the Second World War. My father fought in it and I can just remember some of the aerial action over the Thames estuary when this country was under rocket attack. As I grew up, I became increasingly conscious of the importance of that struggle in preserving the freedoms which we enjoy in this country and the sacrifices that the men and women of Britain had made so that my generation and succeeding ones could go on enjoying them. Some people tragically had been maimed or lost their lives during that conflict as every war memorial throughout the country testifies. It is because the people of this country value our independence and our freedoms so highly that they have been willing to defend them so valiantly over the centuries. Many tyrants have come to rue the day when they threatened us and ignored our history. I have no doubt that the British people will rise to similar challenges in the future.

It is this vital thread of continuity between the past, the present and the future that the Royal British Legion exists to preserve and honour. The heroism of our servicemen and servicewomen in the past and present is a reminder to everyone of the sacrifices made and of their enduring legacy. It can never be forgotten. I am certain that it never will be.

Andrew Rowe MP

My uncle, who won an MC in the First World War, carried with him to his grave the damage done by gas encountered in the trenches. His disappointment when the Second World War broke out was very great and there cannot be a thinking person alive who does not bitterly regret that our human race seems incapable of progressing beyond violence to achieve its short term aims.

Not even the extraordinary shift to almost 90% of war casualties now being found among the civilian population can wake the world to the need to find a better way of resolving its differences. That is why it is so important to remember those who have fought and died in so many conflicts in so many parts of the world and that is also why it is essential that mankind learns to live with one another before we destroy ourselves entirely.

I am always proud to be included in the Remembrance Day services in which the Royal British Legion plays such a leading part and I pray that we may still build a society in which the message of hope through faith can achieve the outcome for which so many have given their lives. Unless we find peace, we shall surely go on finding war and that will mean that all those heroes will have, to some extent, died in vain.

Joyce Shrubbs MBE

I spent the war years in my home County of Bedfordshire. Whilst still a schoolgirl I learned the sadness of war. In August 1940 my brother, Stoker Reginald J. Taylor, was killed. He had survived the terrible journeys across the Channel to bring troops out of Dunkirk and during a recreational football match between the Navy and the Army on the cliffs of Dover (arranged to lighten their spirits) they were mown down by enemy machine-gun fire. My brother, severely wounded, lived only one day. It was harvest time on the farm at home. Farmers usually complain of wet weather at harvest time but in 1940 our harvest was wet with tears.

I could not wait to be old enough to get into uniform and play my part but one had to be 18 for most services so when I read of the Royal Observer Corps looking for volunteers aged 17 and upwards, and I was not far from this age. I volunteered straight away and started my services on my 17th birthday in April 1944 at the Bedford Group Control. The surrounding district was full of Airfields and I recall plotting the vast number of Fortresses leaving their bases early each morning and returning late afternoon to be followed by streams of Lancasters and Halifaxes leaving in the late evening and returning in the early hours of the next morning. Some returned badly damaged and some did not return at all. I remember too, the skies filled with Dakotas and gliders and learned later of the Arnhem landings.

Such sacrifices cannot be forgotten and whilst those young heroes would not wish us always to be morbid and sad, it is right and proper to set aside a day each year to honour their memory and the part they played in achieving our freedom.

I have the opportunity to do this each year with the Royal Observer Corps Association and more regularly in my role as Chairman of the Marston Moreteyne Branch of the Royal British Legion.

Members of the Royal Observer Corps Association look back with pride on their service in the Royal Observer Corps, on the Corps' history and particularly on the part played in the Second World War.

Known as the 'Eyes and Ears' of the Royal Air Force, the Corps maintained a constant watch of the sky, tracking all aircraft, both hostile and friendly, across the Country enabling fighter controllers to bring about interceptions and the destruction of enemy aircraft and to guide many pilots, limping home in distress from their operations over enemy territory, to the nearest home base and in all kinds of weather. The Corps' advice of the approach of enemy aircraft enabled Air Raid Warnings to be sounded and thus gave some measure of protection to the civilian population too. How well the Observer Corps did its job can be deduced from the fact that His Majesty King George VI bestowed the title 'Royal Observer Corps' in 1941.

It is the remembrance of these wartime duties and the dedicated commitment of the Observers to protect their Country that enables members of this Association to march with pride past the Cenotaph on Remembrance Sunday each year remembering also, as they do so, the great sacrifice of others

Kenneth Clarke MP

I was a child during the war myself, but I think it is extremely important that subsequent generations never forget the huge national effort and sacrifice made by the ordinary men and women of the United Kingdom in order to ensure that we would remain a democratic and free society. The war brought to an end Fascism and genocide in Europe. I trust it will prove to be a lasting victory, and that the people of Europe will never fight each other again and will never return to the barbaric forms of government that had caused the warfare.

Winston S. Churchill MP

Well do I remember the intensity of the excitement, joy and surge of relief as I stood, aged 4½ , waving my paper Union Jack amid a crowd half a million strong that thronged The Mall outside Buckingham Palace on VE-Day!

Gillian Shephard MP

I was born in 1940, so my memories of the war are those of a small child living in a remote Norfolk village. One thing I will always remember is standing with my mother in our garden, watching my father walk over the fields with his suitcases, to catch the train back to Dover where he was stationed with the Marines. We were lucky, he came back again, but so many did not, or returned wounded and maimed, even in our own small village. I will always remember too, the celebrations we had for VE Day – a barn dance in a real barn – we all took vases of flowers, mine were marigolds tastefully arranged in a jam jar, and the feeling that we could all breathe again. We owe so much to all those who fought for us in that war, and to those who kept the home fires burning. We must never forget.

ROYAL AIR FORCE
WICKENBY
No1·GROUP BOMBER COMMAND
1942~1945

IN MEMORY OF
ONE THOUSAND AND EIGHTY MEN
OF 12 & 626 SQUADRONS
WHO GAVE THEIR LIVES ON
OPERATIONS FROM THIS AIRFIELD
IN THE OFFENSIVE AGAINST GERMANY
AND THE LIBERATION
OF OCCUPIED EUROPE
·Per ardua ad astra·

The Monument at Royal Air Force Wickenby, in memory of the one thousand and eighty men of 12 and 626 Squadrons who gave their lives during the Second World War. Comic actor Michael Bentine, served with both these units. No 626 Squadron was formed from 'C' Flight of 12(B) Squadron in 1943; and in 1983 No 4626 Squadron inherited the affiliation. During the early 1990s Henry Buckton (the author) joined No 4626 Squadron as an Aero-Med at RAF Lyncham in Wiltshire.
(Photo courtesy The Wickenby Register)

CHAPTER FOUR

MEMORIALS

War memorials are without question our most poignant celebration to the memory of the men and women who died for their country during the wars of this century. They act as our most comprehensive record and link with great historical events. The names listed upon them reflect the communities from which the fallen came. The cenotaphs and memorials in our town centres have no bearing on social status or rank; lieutenant-colonels are listed with privates; air commodores with aircraftmen, and rear-admirals with stokers. Each represented his parish, each represented his country, and ultimately, each made the same sacrifice.

Memorials dedicated to those who fell in the Second World War come in a hundred different guises. Nearly every town in the country has an example of sorts. The main type is an outside cenotaph, or perhaps a cross, quite often in Celtic design, or a stone obelisk, pillar or statue. These are usually set in – to use Paddy Ashdown's words – a place of civic dignity. They might be in the town or market square, main thoroughfare, by the town hall, or in the peaceful settings of a park. Most commonly they are situated in the grounds of the parish church. It is very difficult to differentiate between the two World Wars as most civic war memorials in towns or villages were built as a result of the First World War with the names of those who perished in the Second World War added at a later date. Having said that, those who represent the First World War, who invariably outnumber the World War II fallen, take pride of place, with the later entries being added somewhere to the back, side or base of the monument, or inscribed on specially attached plaques. The other interesting thing here is that the memorials in the villages are often just as – or more – elaborate than those in large towns.

It would be impossible and a bit distracting from the main purpose of this book, to start listing memorials. However, due to their inseperable importance with the theme of Remembrance, it will suffice to mention examples of overall significance to the nation, or the particular services.

Many of the major monuments and cenotaphs were erected on

behalf of the Imperial War Graves Commission, and by far the most important architects were, Charles Holden, Herbert Baker, Sir Reginald Blomfield, and Sir Edwin Lutyens.

In 1919, Lutyens was appointed by Lloyd George to design a monument for the London Peace Celebrations of July that year. A temporary example made of plaster and wood was unveiled on 19 July, with a permanent, construction, which changed very little from the original designs, unveiled on the second anniversary of the armistice in 1920. This monument, is now respected as the British National Memorial, and has come to be known as 'The Cenotaph.' It would also be true to say that its design was to prove more influential than any other monument, which is not hard to understand, in due of the fact that the war it was built to represent, was itself, responsible for more examples than any other conflict, including the Second World War.

As far as the Royal Navy is concerned, the most important examples can be found at Chatham, Plymouth and Portsmouth, designed by Sir Robert Lorimer. All of these were erected following the First World War, but extended by the architect Sir Edward Maufe, and the sculptor Sir Charles Wheeler, after the Second. Lutyens was again responsible for the Merchant Navy Memorial, Tower Hill, London, and Blomfield, the RAF Memorial on Victoria Embankment. Another important, but far more modern monument (1989), is the Royal Air Force and Allied Air Forces of World War II Monument, erected on Plymouth Hoe.

The Army is never as clear cut as the Royal Navy and Royal Air Force, although major monuments have been erected to certain Divisions and Regiments, such as the Guards' Division Memorial in St. James's Park; the Cavalry Memorial in Hyde Park; and the Artillery Memorial. Of course, there are hundreds more, and a good book for those interested in the subject is entitled 'War Memorials' by Alan Borg, the Director-General of the Imperial War Museum. Later in this chapter Alan Borg describes some of the work done by the Imperial War Museum, which is itself, one of our greatest memorials.

Facing page: The Royal Air Force International Air Monument on Plymouth Hoe. Designed by Jim Davis of Plymouth, the monument was unveiled on Sunday 3rd September 1989. (Photo courtesy RAF & Allied Air Forces Monument Service Committee)

From: H.R.H. The Duke of Kent, KG

YORK HOUSE
ST. JAMES'S PALACE
LONDON S.W.1

In my travels as President of the Commonwealth War Graves Commission I have often had cause to reflect on the scale of loss suffered during the two World Wars. The Commission cares for war cemeteries and memorials in no less than 145 countries, where one and three quarter million Commonwealth servicemen and women lie buried or are commemorated on memorials to the missing.

But although such appallingly large numbers are involved, it is always the individual we remember; each one by name. The names, the ages and especially the personal inscriptions chosen by relatives all go to make every headstone and every cemetery a poignant and eloquent testimonial to the human cost of war. When I visit these cemeteries, I am reminded that these were individual human beings; husbands, wives, parents and children.

In our task of commemorating those who gave their lives we strive to make the war cemeteries oases of serenity where visitors may pause to recollect. And we feel certain that in the future, these memorials will remind generations yet to come not only of the suffering of war, of the striving together against a multitude of hardships, but also of the need to work tirelessly for a free and peaceful world.

HRH The Duke of Kent, KG
President
The Commonwealth War Graves Commission

HRH The Duke of Kent KG

President of The Commonwealth War Graves Commission

In my travels as President of the Commonwealth War Graves Commission I have often had cause to reflect on the scale of loss suffered during the two World Wars. The Commission cares for war cemeteries and memorials in no less than 145 countries, where one and three quarter million Commonwealth servicemen and women lie buried or are commemorated on memorials to the missing.

But although such appallingly large numbers are involved, it is always the individual we remember; each one by name. The names, the ages and especially the personal inscriptions chosen by relatives all go to make every headstone and every cemetery a poignant and eloquent testimonial to the human cost of war. When I visit these cemeteries, I am reminded that these were individual human beings; husbands, wives, parents and children.

In our task of commemorating those who gave their lives we strive to make the war cemeteries oases of serenity where visitors may pause to recollect. And we feel certain that in the future, these memorials will remind generations yet to come not only of the suffering of war, of the striving together against a multitude of hardships, but also of the need to work tirelessly for a free and peaceful world.

Max Hastings

When visiting the Commonwealth cemeteries of the two World Wars, I have always been most deeply moved by reading the ages against the names on the headstones. So many of those who lie in France and Italy, North Africa and the Far East, were 18, 19, 20 when they died. At 48, I do not today like to think of myself as an old man. Yet already, I have enjoyed more than twice the life that those men did, and I hope I shall never forget that I owe this to them. My generation is a deeply privileged one, because we have never been called upon to fight and to suffer fearful loss, in the way that our parents and grandparents did. When I researched my own books on the Second World War, I read many letters and diaries written by young soldiers, sailors and airmen, who recognised the likelihood that they would die. Yet most went into battle with a remarkable absence of bitterness or complaint, because they believed that this was their duty – if not to their country or to some great-sounding cause, at least to their "oppo", the man in the next trench or gun turret or cockpit. Duty, dignity and sacrifice are words often cheapened by promiscuous use. Yet they are there in full measure in the Commonwealth War Graves across the world.

The war memorial in Crewkerne of which Paddy Ashdown MP says: 'was not put in some place of civic dignity, but in the middle of a Council estate, where the greatest number of those who died would actually have come from.' (Photo: Henry Buckton)

Paddy Ashdown MP

It was, I think, J.B. Priestley who said "I dislike war memorials – they dispose of the dead too easily".

That may be, for some, an understandable emotion for those who lived through the terrors of the great wars and knew personally both the suffering and the people who died.

But for us – as for the vast majority of those of the war generations who put them up with such reverence and care for position and design, our war memorials are the means by which we are called not to forget.

I think of the memorial which stands as a proud sentinel on the edge of Ham Hill – at Stoke-sub-Hamdon in my Yeovil constituency – watching over the Somerset levels and the main road which still, at this point, follows the ancient line of the Fosse Way and recalling to every native and passing traveller, that their enjoyment of liberty and this countryside was bought at the cost of English men's lives.

Or the war memorial in Crewkerne, which, presumably deliberately, was not put in some place of civic dignity, but in the middle of a Council estate, where the greatest number of those who died would actually have come from.

Or the memorial in Yeovil itself, standing proud and honoured every year in the Borough to act as a daily reminder to all who pass of the debt we owe to people whose names we can read but whose faces have long ago passed, with the lives they gave up, out of recall, but not out of remembrance.

Our war memorials are at once reminders that much of our good fortune is owed to others and warnings of what happens if we do not understand the lessons of the mistakes they had to pay for.

It is right to remember and celebrate them in this book.

Sir Alec Guinness

When I was a boy and most people wore hats no man would think of passing The Cenotaph without raising his hat or saluting the fallen in some way. That is a very rare sight now; for many The Cenotaph has become just a large stone obstruction to London's impatient traffic. Perhaps those who instruct the young could be persuaded to instill in them some sense of history; or maybe it would be possible to suggest to all under fifty years of age that every now and then, when passing a village or small-town memorial, they might pause for a moment to read the names engraved on it. The names might mean nothing to them, of course, but the readers could reflect that those men and women were probably not very different from themselves.

The Most Reverend George Carey

The Archbishop of Canterbury

Our country owes its much vaunted freedom to those who fought so bravely for us. In nearly every Anglican Church of this land there are tablets to the glorious fallen of two world wars. We are proud to have them there. They will remain as powerful reminders of young men and women whose lives were cut short for each of us.

Lambeth Palace London SE1 7JU

ARCHBISHOP OF CANTERBURY'S CONTRIBUTION TO THE
ROYAL BRITISH LEGION'S GOLDEN BOOK OF REMEMBRANCE

I saw the Second World War through the eyes of a child. I was
four when the war broke out. At first it seemed fun and even
exciting. I recall looking from a bomb shelter at the night
skies watching our searchlights hunt for German bombers. I
recall too hearing the sound of the sinister doodle bugs. But
later its discomforts and horror came home to me with
considerable force. I remember school friends who did not turn
up for school because they were injured or killed the night
before. Three times, my brothers and sisters and I were
evacuated and experienced the bewilderment of unfamiliar places
and the strange country accents of strangers who befriended us.

Those experiences taught me the truth about war. I came to
view it, not as fun or exciting, but as something that always
leaves scars and the painful memories of those whose lives were
ended abruptly or were left in ruins through the evils of
combat. For this reason we should never forget the lessons of
war. There are times when evil has to be fought, but we must
not underestimate the cost involved.

Our country owes its much vaunted freedom to those who fought
so bravely for us. In nearly every Anglican Church of this
land there are tablets to the glorious fallen of two world
wars. We are proud to have them there. They will remain as
powerful reminders of young men and women whose lives were cut
short for each one of us.

+ George Cantuar

Victor Bonham-Carter

Whatever form a memorial takes, be it a monument, a book, or a school scholarship, it must be a true and constant reminder of why a war was fought, of its consequences, and of the sacrifices involved.

Ian Carmichael

War memorials are scattered throughout our islands. They range in stature from Lutyens' impressive Cenotaph in Whitehall and the magnificent Scottish memorial in Edinburgh Castle, through grand sculptures in city centres, to modest stone crosses and obelisks in tiny villages that bear only a handful of names. Each and every one is, in my view, as important to our heritage as the Palace of Westminster.

It is right that all those who made the supreme sacrifice for their country – our country – should be remembered in perpetuity. These memorials – even those commemorating the fallen in wars that were fought before I was born – always have a profound effect upon me. They make me stop, think and, where possible, remember – and that is good. It is right. It is proper. It is what they are there for.

Remembrance Day itself, 11th November (how potent the two minutes silence was when it was observed annually at 11am on that date), and the parades and ceremonies that take place during Remembrance Week are, for me, highly emotional experiences. That too is good, right and proper. For a few brief moments one is reminded: one is made to reflect on those men – Tom, Dick and Harry, many of whom died at the ages my grand children are today. Men who never lived long enough to have children of their own, let alone grandchildren. Without the sacrifice they made, the last half century would have seen a very different Britain to the one we share today.

These memorials are not, as has been suggested by some, a glorification of war. They are a sober reminder of its miseries and pain. If we cannot learn from our history, then their blood will have been shed in vain.

Long may the spirit of remembrance remain in our islands – we fortunate souls who remain to enjoy the benefits that their sacrifice secured.

Don Foster MP

There are few things in life more moving than visiting the cemeteries of Flanders or Normandy. The serried ranks of tombestones provide an indelible reminder of the cost of war. Part of the impact stems from the sheer numbers of the fallen buried there. No less moving, however, are the memorials in every city, town, village and community in Britain, commemorating those who died serving their country. Fathers and sons, uncles and brothers paid the supreme sacrifice. Not only shall we remember them – the nation's war memorials ensure that we cannot forget them.

David Heathcoat-Amory MP

Like any MP, I spend many hours in village and town halls, attending meetings and addressing gatherings on various issues. Often, when interest in the proceedings flags somewhat, my eye wanders to the Remembrance plaque on the wall with its roll of honour of English men who fought in the wars of this century. I feel in some way that I am representing them too and am determined to keep alive the traditions of free speech and national liberty for which they died.

I am glad they are honoured in the thousands of war memorials throughout the country: a reminder that even the dullest parish meeting takes place under the freedom for which they gave their lives.

Sir Ranulph Fiennes

Although Exmoor is one of England's remotest corners, the memorials and plaques throughout the region honour the many local people who gave the ultimate sacrifice during the two great conflicts of this century. This sacrifice was made in the name of liberty and justice. Basic human rights that were just as important on the quiet moors of this country, as they were in the humiliated cities of the continent. Infact, these rugged hills played their own part at home, fielding the 1st Battalion of the Home Guard. This was the only Home Guard unit to which the War Office issued cavalry equipment. Its mounted patrols kept watch over Exmoor, the Brendon Hills and the coast. Two men from the battalion were killed before the conflict was finally over.

In celebrating those who died we should never forget the burden that was placed on the community at home. Nowhere was this burden greater than in the harsh, bleak hills of Exmoor. Their continued management was a memorial to those that remained behind.

PENTLAND SOUTH POLE

Patron : His Royal Highness The Prince of Wales
Organisers : Charles Burton and Oliver Shepard
Polar Adviser : Sir Vivian Fuchs F R S
Leader : Sir Ranulph Fiennes Bt D Sc
Science Leader and Team Member : Dr Michael Stroud
UK Base Propagation : Morag and Laurence Howell

MS
MULTIPLE SCLEROSIS

To raise funds for
THE MULTIPLE SCLEROSIS SOCIETY

Although Exmoor is Somerset's remotest corner, the memorials and plaques throughout the region honour the many local people who gave the ultimate sacrifice during the two great conflicts of this century. This sacrifice was made in the name of liberty and justice. Basic human rights that were just as important on the quiet moors of this county, as they were in the humiliated cities of the continent. Infact, these rugged hills played their own part at home, fielding the 1st Battalion of the Home Guard. This was the only Home Guard unit to which the War Office issued cavalry equipment. Its mounted patrols kept watch over Exmoor, the Brendon Hills and the coast. Two men from the battalion were killed before the conflict was finally over.

In celebrating those who died we should never forget the burden that was placed on the community at home. Nowhere was this burden greater than in the harsh, bleak hills of Exmoor. Their continued management was a memorial to those that remained behind.

Ranulph Fiennes
March 1983

TO COMPLETE THE FIRST CROSSING OF ANTARCTICA ON FOOT

Above: The War Cemetery at Singapore. (Photo courtesy Lord Chalfont)

*Below and facing page: The War Cemetery at the Bridge on the River Kwai.
(Photos courtesy Lord Chalfont)*

The Lord Chalfont OBE MC PC

As I travel around the world on business, half a century after the end of the Second World War, I often take a little time off to visit the memorials to the soldiers, sailors and airmen who laid down their lives in that terrible conflict.

I have spent many moments of reflection and meditation in those silent places – in the green, tropical fields beside the Bridge on the River Kwai; in the barren sands of the Western Desert; or in the beautifully tended cemetery, bright with hibiscus and bougainvillea on a hill in Singapore, looking across the sparkling white city to the sea. Of course, many others have died in battle since the Second World War, and some of them are remembered in the simple garden in Korea, near to the place where British infantrymen fought so heroically at Imjin. Here Korean school children are brought to tend the rose garden and pay their respects to the foreign soldiers who came to their country and never went home.

There are two memorials which, for obvious reasons, mean more to me than most others. One is a simple, unpretentious monument in South Africa, decorated with a wreath of everlasting flowers, where an officer and six soldiers of my own Regiment, the Twenty Fourth of Foot, were awarded the Victoria Cross for their defence of the hospital at Rorke's Drift; and the other is at Kohima in Assam, for it was in Burma that I left many of the friends of my youth and many of my comrades in the same Regiment.

Although we did not take part in the battles at Imphal and Kohima – we were in another part of the jungle – the inscription on the Kohima memorial speaks for all those who died in battle: 'When you go back, Tell them of us and say, For your tomorrow, We gave our today".

We remember our dead not to glorify war, the least civilised of human activities, but in the hope that their courage and self sacrifice will inspire future generations to believe that there are values and ideals that are, when all else fails, worth fighting for and even dying for.

Lord Harding of Petherton

My father, the late Field Marshal Lord Harding, was born and brought up in South Petherton. I now live in Langport and so I have a special feeling for the Sedgemoor area of Somerset. I pass the War Memorial at Huish Episcopi nearly every day and always admire it. The marble tablet in High Ham church engraved with the names of the two sons of Robert and Rose Mead, their only children, who were both killed in the First World War, is especially poignant. I never fail to notice it when I go to services there.

Henry Buckton has done readers a service in reminding them of the supreme sacrifice made by so many in two World Wars, so that we the survivors and descendants could live in freedom.

The war memorial at Huish Episcopi admired daily by Lord Harding, whose father was the late Field Marshal Lord Harding of Petherton. (Photo: Henry Buckton)

Mark Robinson MP

Memorials are to be found all over my constituency and not always in the likely places. Some contain touching inscriptions and it is always worth taking time to read a Remembrance plaque.

The message reminds us not just of individual sacrifice, but of the burden placed on the entire community. Constituency interests take an MP into many quiet corners, but the names will often indicate the families which have played for so long a part in village life.

Lord Armstrong of Ilminster

As we go about our peaceable and customary occasions, we tend to take our war memorials and those whose memories they recall for granted, and to lose sight of the fact that we owe the quality of our freedom and much that we value in our way of life to those who gave their lives in two World Wars, and indeed in other conflicts, to preserve them. Ilminster and virtually every parish in its neighbourhood has each its own memorial. Here as elsewhere the memorials remind us how many people lost their lives in the service of their country, and what gaps they left in the communities and families from which they came.

Sir Jerry Wiggin TD MP

Memorials are a tangible way of reflecting the natural human desire to respect and remember. They vary in character and location but frequently stir thoughts of gallant deeds performed by our ancestors in defence of our liberty. I recall the beautifully designed War Memorial in the Falkland Islands facing out over Stanley Sound with the names of all who fell in the recent conflict with the Argentinians and just across the road, the Memorial to the fallen in the Battle of the South Atlantic which, at the beginning of the First World War, saw the defeat of the German fleet with the loss of many thousands of lives on both sides.

On the more simple and modest memorial at the church in Axbridge, where I live, there are monuments to the many hundreds of citizens of that town who have contributed to its life over many centuries and as well, there is the quite simple memorial to those who died in the Barsle air crash, many of whom came from Axbridge.

The Commonwealth War Graves Commission do a wonderful job in maintaining memorials to the fallen in both Great Wars and I have been privileged to see their work in places as far apart as the Falkland Islands, New Guinea, Gallipoli and in many parts of Europe.

Sir Edward du Cann KBE

After the 1914 war the Peace Committee in Wellington raised a fund to build a war memorial in the town. On it are recorded the names of 178 men who fell; and now, mercifully, fewer names from the 1939–45 war. This followed the precedent of a century earlier when a memorial was erected on the Blackdown Hills to the great Duke and the heroes of the Peninsular and Waterloo battles. Wellington folk, all our history long, have lived and fought and sometimes died for our beliefs. We followed the wise King Alfred and Monmouth's tragic rebels in the cause of freedom; in my father's and my own generation we defeated tyranny in Europe and the Far East.

We will remember the example of our forebears, and forever. From their firm hands we inherit the torch of freedom and we keep it safe. So we make our contribution to England's history in our own time. That is our tradition. Our local memorials confirm our dedication to it.

Colonel Geoffrey Walter Luttrell

Throughout our country we find war memorials commemorating those killed in the two great and terrible wars of this century. It matters not whether a memorial is a simple plaque containing one name or a noble stone monument inscribed with the many names recording the sacrifices made by the citizens of our larger towns – each is cared for with pride and gratitude by those of us whose names do not appear on what are truly Rolls of Honour.

HRH Prince Bernhard of the Netherlands

Provided by The RAF and Allied Air Forces Monument. Committee

As Honorary Air Marshal I still feel very much part of the RAF. This monument has an added importance to me, as it also gives credit to all those airmen from allied forces that co-operated in the massive and daunting tasks during the Second World War. As you well know the Netherlands armed forces provided a great number of squadrons to the RAF both in fighter and bomber commands. The squadron numbering in the Netherlands both in The Royal Netherlands Airforce and the Royal Netherlands Naval Air Arm reflect these ancient ties. I will therefore join you today in thoughts and spirits to commemorate those that gave their lives some 50 years ago.

Soestdijk Palace

To the distinguished guests present at this ceremony:

I am honoured that the organizing committee invited me to take part in a commemorative ceremony today here in Plymouth. Other commitments, however, preclude me from joining you.

As Honorary Air Marshal I still feel very much part of the RAF. This monument has an added importance to me, as it also gives credit to all those airmen from allied forces that cooperated in the massive and daunting tasks during WW II. As you well know the Netherlands armed forces provided a great number of squadrons to the RAF both in fighter and bomber commands. The squadron numbering in The Netherlands both in The Royal Netherlands Airforce and the Royal Netherlands Naval Air Arm reflect these ancient ties. I will therefore join you today in thoughts and spirits to commemorate those that gave their lives some 50 years ago.

Prince of the Netherlands

Alan Borg
Director General of the Imperial War Museum

There are many people who question the need for war museums. War, they say, is a dangerous topic; our aim should be to forget. Museums can only serve to glorify the violence of past ages – even, perhaps, condition us to more violence in the future. Others take a different view. It is important, they say, to remember what has happened in the past, perhaps so that we may avoid the same mistakes in the future.

Both of these views give an unrealistic impression of what a museum can actually achieve. No war museum is either going to cause or to prevent any war in the future – we work on the margins of society and our opinions are not asked for by decision-making politicians or front-line soldiers. Our role is to remember and, just as importantly, to understand – to understand historical circumstances and to understand human behaviour, as a means of understanding ourselves.

The way in which we try and achieve these aims has changed over the last decade and will continue to change in the future, as world circumstances and public perceptions change. War and the public attitude to it is very different in the 1990s from what it was in the 1920s or the 1950s. A war museum that is not alert to these changes and does not reflect them in its displays will soon appear obsolete, without contemporary significance.

When the Imperial War Museum was founded in 1920 its main purpose was to commemorate the effort and sacrifice of all who had fought and died in the Great War. This commemorative purpose was reinforced when the Museum's terms of references were extended to include the Second World War. It was seen as a Museum to which veterans would come bringing, first their children, then their grandchildren. However, it has been clear for more than a decade that our role must change. The veterans of the First World War have almost gone; those of the Second World War are growing older and becoming fewer. For today's children these two World Wars are as much part of history as the wars of Napoleon or even Julius Caesar.

However, we have not abandoned our original purpose –

still central to our role is the commemoration of the bravery and sacrifice of those who died, to remember that for our tomorrow they gave their today. What has changed is that we cannot assume any special knowledge or interest on the part of our visitors. Our aim is to educate in the broadest sense and to make people think, so that the cataclysmic events of the 20th century remain relevant to future generations, and will help people to learn for the present by remembering the past.

London's Imperial War Museum is dedicated to the remembrance of those who fell in the two world wars. Its constantly evolving displays and exhibitions help to remind us of the sacrifice that was made by so many. (Photo courtesy Imperial War Museum)

CHAPTER FIVE

THE MUSIC OF MEMORY

Lord Craig of Radley

Recent experiences of war – I was Chief of the Defence Staff during the Gulf conflict – are portrayed all too vividly on our television screens and in the daily newspapers. But horrifying as these scenes may be, it is only when you imagine how even more terrible they would have been if we had been shown the scale of human suffering and death which occured between 1939 and 1945.

Our country must never forget the debt we owe to so many of our finest young men and women in those years. Their sacrifice has made it possible for those who followed to enjoy an ever increasing standard of living and freedom from oppression.

In this chapter we shall be looking at the way in which the media and entertainment worlds, have created their own chapter in terms of remembrance and have sustained it down through the years. Music, cinema, television, literature and poetry, are all used to remind us of the sacrifice which was made.

Perhaps one of the most instantaneous aids to Remembrance is music. Music in all its varied formatts can trigger off the most detailed memories of something which happened a very long time ago. Very often we hear a particular piece of music that stirs a long forgotten emotion. Those who did not live through the Second World War have a very strong impression of its musical accompaniment. Whenever a director sets out these days to make a film about England during the wars years, especially its second half, part of its formula is the inclusion of the distinctive music from the era. Consequently, younger people think of the war years as the 'Age of Swing.'

Swing music was only a very small part of the varied musical scene at that time but it seems to have left the strongest impression. Much of its influence arrived with the American army of occupation, who set up camp all around the country. Much of its success is credited to one man, Glen Miller. Of course, Miller had been a band leader in America for many years before the war, and Swing music itself had been around since the late 1920s.

The first Vl rocket hit London on 10 June 1944. Five days later, the capital was hit by Swing, with the arrival of Captain Glenn Miller, who had been sent to England to entertain American and British troops with his army band. From that time until the end of the war this American innovation became very familiar at concerts and on the radio, not just entertaining the troops, but the entire nation. Glenn Miller's legacy to remembrance in Britain was cemented by the fact that he died during his tour here. This in a way, made an entire style of music a memorial to the memory of one man. On 15 December 1944, after only a short time in the country, the C-64 Norseman light aircraft on which Miller was a passenger, disappeared over the English Channel.

There were other great artistes associated with the 'Age of Swing', who although now, almost entirely forgotten will undoubtedly be remembered by those who lived through the war years. There were people like Benny Goodman, Tommy Dorsey, Count Basie, Woody Herman and Artie Shaw, and artistes such as Frank Sinatra, Perry Como, Jimmy Rushing, Ella Fitzgerald, Peggy Lee, Doris Day and Bing Crosby, who have remained household names by the constant re-runs of period movies.

Long before we had been invaded by the Americans, many great English entertainers had already become associated with the Second World War, and the mere mention of their names, is in itself an act of Remembrance. Who among you could hear the names Dame Vera Lynn and Gracie Fields, without automatically thinking of the Second World War?

With the war came the creation of ENSA (Entertainments National Service Association). No longer did people have to go out to see a show, the shows came to them. Concerts, concert parties, plays and cinema entertainment were provided wherever British forces deployed. The following names may be unfamiliar to many of us, but to our parents and grandparents they were certainly not: Jack Hilton, Will Hay, Harry Lauder, Dame Sybil Thorndike, Miss Irene Vanbrugh, Lewis Casson, Bronson Albery, Jack Waller, Firth Shephard, Mr Eames, Ernest Irving, Billy

Cotton, Henry Hall, Geraldo and Edward Jones. There were many others whose contributions to ENSA, created a special place for the world of entertainment in terms of Remembrance.

When we are reminded of certain things in our past, by hearing a piece of music on the radio, it's usually to do with the moment we met someone special, an achievement, such as passing an exam or our driving test, our college years, and things of this nature. Quite often when the war generations are reminded by a piece of music, it was the last time they saw their husband or father alive, when a neighbour, friend or member of their family was killed during the blitz. And naturally, few people could ever forget VE-Day and the music which filled their hearts with a tremendous sense of relief.

Many famous movie stars abandoned the glamour of Hollywood to enlist in the armed forces at the outbreak of war. In 1942 David Niven was released for 'special duty', after a break from acting for three years. The 'special duty' was to star in a film called *The First of the Few*. Niven played Wing Commander Geoffrey Crisp in a film backed by the Royal Air Force, intended to inspire the nation. Because of its timing, the film appears to be a propaganda exercise. 50 years on, 'The First of the Few' and the thousands of films and television programmes which have been made about the Second World War, keep alive the memories and the debt we owe. Even today, the Second World War remains an important subject for movies and documentaries alike. Handled correctly, by skilful directors and actors, the young of today are perpetually reminded of their inheritaance and the generation that bought it.

Television has become very important to the act of Remembrance. Millions of people every year, old and young alike, take an interest in the Festival of Remembrance and the protocol at the Cenotaph. Due to the coverage given to these occasions by television and radio companies, and newspapers, Remembrance Sunday has become a fixed item in the annual traditions and ceremony of the nation. Television also helps us to remember through its coverage of special remembrance ceremonies, such as those to mark the 50th anniversary of D-Day.

David Dimbleby

On a number of occasions I have been privileged to be the BBC's television commentator on Remembrance Sunday watching the faces of those on parade. Most moving for me was the day I worked out that if all the Allied dead of both world wars were to march past the Cenotaph four abreast, as the veterans do, the front of the procession would be in London while the rear would still be in Edinburgh.

It was as vivid a reminder that every family in Britain and many families in the Commonwealth were touched by those great events and each in its own way made sacrifices so that Hitler and Germany could be defeated.

Probably the most consistent and massive contribution towards remembrance, made by any of the different art forms, is literature. During the Second World War, and over the 50 years since it's close, tens of thousands of books have been dedicated to the subject. As well as historical accounts of the war in general, its battles and combatants, there are stories of romance, intrigue, and adventure. There have been comic strips and magazines and block buster novels. Each in its own way, is an act of remembrance. In recent years, due to the succession of anniversaries we have seen, the subject has again been very fashionable. I hope that this book itself is an act of remembrance. Although each of these works helps to keep alive the memory of the Second World War, they are not necessarily intended to honour the memory of those who fell, or to give thanks for the legacy which they entrusted to us. Infact, in my experience this is all too rarely the case. Yes, we need to remember great historical events and appreciate military strategy. The idea behind this book is not to glorify war, quite the contrary. Most of those who fought were not military men, they were volunteers who believed in truth, justice and liberty and who loved their country, their families and their homes. Or they were conscripted into the armed forces, to fight a war, which would ensure that their children and grandchildren would not have to fight again for 50 years.

In one of the major novels of 1994 *A Parliamentary Affair*, by Edwina Currie, an entire chapter is set during Remembrance

Sunday. Although the incident in question ends in frivolity, it is a poignant and very moving example of the way in which modern literature can be employed in the spirit, that our own book attempts to emulate. With the kind permission of Mrs Currie, and Hodder & Stoughton Publishers, the following is an extract from the novel.

Edwina Currie MP

From: A Parliamentary Affair

One service all year stood out, for Elaine as for many MPs: Remembrance Day. Her constituency was recruiting territory for several regiments. Each year there seemed to be a new smattering of young soldiers on parade, war-weary from the Gulf or Bosnia, or with the watchful air of those who have served in Ulster.

The grand old organ boomed out powerful rumbling notes as the congregation rose solemnly to its feet amid wholesale clearing of throats. The weather had been damp and the cathedral was not yet warm; the standard-bearers were blue with cold and the Brownies were shivering. Lusty hymn-singing would make everyone feel better.

After the hymn, a young woman infantry officer, top cadet in her year at Sandhurst, stepped forward to the lectern. In the front row her parents swelled with pride. Necks craned as the girl stood calmly in her smart green uniform, blood-red poppy at her breast. There was something about a woman dressed like that, incongruous but enormously sexy. Men, confused, lowered their eyes.

I heard a voice from heaven, saying unto me, Write, from henceforth blessed are the dead which die in the Lord: Even so, saith the Spirit, for they rest from their labours.

Elaine looked around her. Of course she should be concentrating on the service but her constituents were much more interesting. Mostly over middle age, comfortable and well upholstered, peaceable and kindly. Once a year they chose to remember the cost of war without mawkishness or embarrassment.

The president of the British Legion, now nearly eighty, headed for the microphone. As a young man he had served with Montgomery in North Africa, losing an eye when the tank was blown from under him and all his mates killed. Medals clanked on his chest and his long lower lip was not quite under control as he started reading the Memorial of the Dead, his voice shaking with emotion.

> Remember, O Lord, all those brave and true,
> who have died the death of honour . . . .
> to whom it was given to lay down their lives
> in the cause of Freedom and Justice . . . .

Elaine felt suddenly very moved. Had she been required at that moment to make a comment out loud she could not have done it. That Europe was free at all was thanks to the sacrifices of such people and their comrades.

The cathedral waited. It was eleven o'clock. High in the medieval belltower Great Tom tolled as everyone silently counted. As the last reverberations died away the president drew himself up to his full height and spoke very slowly:

> Age shall not weary them, nor the years condemn.
> At the going down of the sun and in the morning,
> We will remember them.

Nigel Boswood had decided to attend the televised service at the Cenotaph in Whitehall. Why not? As a Cabinet Minister he would have been in the second row behind the Prime Minister and Leader of the Opposition, near the Queen in her regulation black. Now he was at the back. He was well wrapped up against the bitter wind, an extra-large poppy firmly pinned to his coat, neck muffled in the black scarf kept for this event year by year.

The war itself did not mean much to Nigel. Only six years old when it broke out, he had promptly been shipped off to relatives in Canada with his sister. He remembered the outward journey on board the great cruise liner, with deck tennis, a swimming pool and children's shows, with the greatest enjoyment, which coloured his whole recollection of the following innocent years, until his return to a cheerless English prep school after VE Day. From the train, then, he was shocked at the devastation of Liverpool: a three-legged dog limping across bomb sites near the flattened Edge Hill goods depot, the yawning gaps in street after street in Wavertree where houses had received a direct hit, their inhabitants pulled out in pieces. The images stayed with him. The desire to do his bit became a driving force in his politics.

Behind him the Regimental Band of the Blues and Royals tinkled and hissed as stops were flexed, spittle discreetly emptied from trombones and bright brass raised to stiff lips. A gentle drum roll led the congregation into a very British hymn. Nigel joined in proudly. So what if God was an internationalist?

> Of every clime and coast,
> O hear us for our native land
> The land we love the most . . . .

Tessa Muncastle tried to stop herself shivering and wondered if putting her gloved hands in her pockets would be too disrespectful. Hampshire might be in the lush south but half an hour in a November wind had penetrated all her defences. Next to her stood the standard-bearer of the Women's Royal British Legion, a stout lady in a navy-blue uniform, big feet in sensible lace-up shoes planted wide apart, huge white leather gloves like catcher's mitts on both hands, the Legion hat jammed unbudgeably on her head with several hatpins. The standard itself, having been paraded around the town, was propped up beside her.

'Terrible, isn't it?'

Tessa realised the standard-bearer was commiserating with her. She smiled ruefully. 'It is a bit chilly. Wish I'd worn something warmer.'

The woman leaned forward with a cheery grin. 'long johns, that's what I wear,' she hissed. 'Borrowed me old man's, the short-leg ones. Look.'

To Tessa's consternation she lifted her skirt and showed the tell-tale white ribbing covering her ample thighs, like prepared hams in a butcher's. Tessa coloured in embarrassment.

The woman returned to attention. The MP's wife was nice but a bit po-faced. This was a solemn occasion, but there was always room for a giggle. Do her good to enjoy herself occasionally. Him too – took himself so seriously these days now he was a Minister.

Andrew held himself rigidly straight on the podium as
the rest of the parade drew near, a large poppy
prominently displayed in his buttonhole. Next to him
stood the rural dean in flowing voluminous red, his
unaccustomed portliness suggesting layers of fortification
underneath.

Frowning slightly, Tessa peered down the wide street in
the direction of the martial music. In the absence of the
county's regiments in Bosnia the local Territorials, the
reserves, had volunteered to put on a good show, especially
as the MP would be present. First the Scout band came into
view, boys of different ages and sizes, struggling to keep
step, supported by Guides and Cubs. Behind the band
came the Terriers in khaki.

It was then that Tessa caught sight of the mascot and her
heart sank. It was a large white billy-goat with an evil face,
its horns waving dangerously. The troop secretary had
shampooed it for the occasion and caparisoned the
creature sumptuously in TA colours. Pulling hard, it was
leering and skittering out of step in the front row under
the partial control of the commandant, Mr Bulstrode the
retired banker, who was red-faced from the effort of
holding the brute back. Mr Bulstrode was both out of his
area and a little out of his depth. There was no point in
hassling people to attend a parade in nearby Milton if its
MP was missing, as well he might be after all that fuss. A
proper march-past needed a distinguished character to
take the salute. Muncastle was nothing much, but as one of
Her Majesty's new Ministers he would have to do. As long
as this ghastly beast behaved.

As the groups approached the podium the goat began to
scent people. That meant food: sweets, crisps, chips.
Getting away would be difficult, for the man was holding
tight. The parade stopped and the band rested, at ease.
The animal stood balefully eyeing the crowd, head up, as
all fell silent.

The goat felt Mr Bulstrode's grip slacken minutely.

Just at that moment the Scouts put cornets to lips and in
undignified mistune blasted out the Last Post. The goat,
startled, jumped off all fours, jerked its head back, found
itself free, looked around wildly and then made a bee-line

for a half-eaten chocolate bar sticking out of the drum major's pocket. The crowd scattered from its path with yelps and squeals as all semblance of dignity collapsed. Moving remarkably fast, the billy clattered towards its objective. Grasping the chocolate in protruding yellow teeth it began to gobble quickly, but had not counted on the angry youngster. In furious retaliation he lifted the drum with a yell and crashed it down on the goat's head, splitting the drumskin with a loud twang and leaving the rim and remains encircling the animal's neck. The beast's amber eyes rolled unfocused; then, as instinct took over, it put its splendid horned head down and charged the boy full tilt.

In an instant there was uproar as the big goat, somewhat hampered by its unusual collar, careered on into the crowd, which scattered in all directions, screaming and laughing. Bulstrode waded in, scrabbling in the road for the leather lead, but the animal was not about to relinquish its new-found freedom. With a skip it dodged neatly out of the way. Mothers snatched babies from prams and clutched them to their breasts, old ladies in terror pressed themselves flat against shop windows, young men came out of pubs and ran around whooping. The hefty goat, no mean beast, chocolate wrapper still hanging from its lips, charged aimlessly and vengefully about. The lady standard-bearer, a broad grin on her weatherbeaten face, deftly moved Tessa out of the way. On the podium Andrew and the rural dean watched helplessly; once it was apparent that normal service was not to be restored, the two relaxed and joined in the general merriment.

At last the tiring goat was headed off by a group of Scouts and Terriers and was cornered down by the tandoori restaurant. Mr Ali was standing in the doorway, wiping his hands on a tea-towel. A panting heap of humanity and smelly long-haired goat greeted him as Bulstrode, face livid, strode up and took the leash again.

'I could make use of the animal, sir, should you wish to dispose of it,' Mr Ali said helpfully.

'I'll be in touch tomorrow,' responded the goat's minder grimly.

Poetry is another media which has been used to remember the two world wars. The example I have used to end this chapter, was not written by one of our great bards, but was discovered on the dead body of an American soldier, killed in action in North Africa in 1944. Framed in a little corner of remembrance in a quiet village church near to the author's home, it reads:

Look God, I have never spoken to you,
and now I want to say How do you do.
You see God, they told me you did not exist,
and I, like a fool, believed all this.
Last night, from a shell hole I saw your sky,
I figured they had told me a lie.
Had I taken time before to see things you had made,
I'd sure have known they weren't calling a spade a spade.
I wonder God if you would shake my poor hand?
Somehow I feel you would understand.
Strange I had come to this hellish place,
before I had time to see your face.
Well, I guess there isn't much more to say,
but I'm glad, God, that I met you today.
The zero hour will soon be here,
but I'm not afraid to know that you're near.
The signal has come, I shall soon have to go.
I like you lots, this I want you to know.
I am sure this will be a horrible fight.
Who knows? I may come to your house tonight.
Though I wasn't friendly to you before,
I wonder, God, if you'd wait at your door.
Look, I'm shedding tears, me shedding tears.
Oh! I wish I'd known you these long, long years.
Well I have to go now, dear God, goodbye,
but now that I've met you, I'm not scared to die.

CHAPTER SIX

REMEMBRANCE THROUGH THE CHURCH

The Most Reverend George Carey
The Archbishop of Canterbury

I saw the Second World War through the eyes of a child. I was four when the war broke out. At first it seemed fun and even exciting. I recall looking from a bomb shelter at the night skies watching our searchlights hunt for German bombers. I recall too hearing the sound of the sinister doodle bugs. But later its discomforts and horror came home to me with considerable force. I remember school friends who did not turn up for school because they were injured or killed the night before. Three times, my brothers and sisters and I were evacuated and experienced the bewilderment of unfamiliar places and the strange country accents of strangers who befriended us.

Those experiences taught me the truth about war. I came to view it, not as fun or exciting, but as something that always leaves scars and the painful memories of those whose lives were ended abruptly or were left in ruins through the evils of combat. For this reason we should never forget the lessons of war. There are times when evil has to be fought, but we must not underestimate the cost involved.

Cardinal Basil Hume
The Archbishop of Westminster

We must never be allowed to forget the debt that we owe to so many men and women who served King and Country 50 years ago.

Every day we must constantly remember them and quite especially those who made the supreme sacrifice on behalf of the rest of us.

If, in my own way, I try to build up as a churchman what

Pope Paul VI called 'the civilisation of love', I recognise this as only being possible because of the freedom that we enjoy as a result of what was done by so many brave men and women.

I would like to see the Two Minute Silence on November 11 restored throughout the Nation. It was not only a constant reminder of the past, but helped us to focus our minds on the importance of peace in our day.

The Most Reverend John Habgood
The Archbishop of York

One of my main recollections of the War is of the wonderful variety of people who came to live in our house. First it was evacuees from the East End of London who arrived at the beginning of the phoney war, but soon got bored and went home. They were followed by a don from Cambridge, who was doing something mysterious at Bletchley Park. He used to annoy my father by coming down to dinner in his bedroom slippers. I only discovered very recently that his job as a German scholar was to interpret the significance of the messages decoded by Ultra through his knowledge of German psychology.

Then there was the mysterious Naval Commander who lived with his wife in our attic rooms, and who, as we learnt after the war, had been working on the beams along which our bombers flew on their raids over Germany.

Towards the end of the war our house was continuously occupied by bright young society girls who disappeared to Bletchley Park at odd hours of the day and night, and who were continually being rung up by boyfriends. My own sister and sister-in-law were at that stage also working at Bletchley Park, ferrying messages about German submarines to the Admiralty.

Apart from the occasional bomb it was a fairly quiet war for a teenager growing up in a country town. Looking back now I can see that, far from being on the periphery, we were in the centre of things. That is one of the fascinating and frightening truths about war. What is seen is only the tip of the iceberg. And each of us witnesses only a tiny fraction of the suffering too – which I suppose is just as well for our sanity.

The Right Reverend James Thompson
The Bishop of Bath and Wells

It is significant that the Christian faith has, at the heart of its worship, an act of remembrance. We remember the love, courage and generosity of one who gave His life for humankind. War memorials are, in a way, local shrines of remembrance where we give thanks for people who gave themselves and sacrificed their lives for the wider benefit of humankind. Nations who forget their past are always in danger of losing their identity and worse, going down the same old evil roads that the human race has travelled before. We hear at the moment such disturbing phrases as 'ethnic cleansing' and we see neo-fascist revival in many countries in Europe. It therefore is especially important in this year of the anniversary of Wilfred Owen's death that we should remember both the horrors and the sacrifice of war and recommit ourselves to peace and justice as the will of God and our duty and goal as His children. This book will be a guide to such remembrance.

The Right Reverend John Richardson MA
The Bishop of Bedford

I belonged to that group of men who were called up for National Service, right at the end of Conscription, spending most of my time with the Gunners in Malaya.

Despite some of the things we had to do, it was one of the happiest periods of a happy life. Comradeship, a communal sense of purpose, an important job of work to do and much more beside. Had I not been given a place at University I would have signed on.

A few years later I saw military service from the other end as an Honorary Legion Padre, a position which I held for nearly thirty years. I counted it a privilege to be allowed to share in occasional amounts of splendour, but more importantly perhaps to be with people to whom war had been a nightmare – sharing in some small measure their often continuing sense of loss and hurt. Somehow it seemed just here that Faith could often speak most powerfully.

Although I am no longer an official padre I admire the Royal British Legion enormously, and I wish it well in its on-going work amongst so many whose need is still so important.

The Right Reverend Mark Santer
The Bishop of Birmingham

For me the Second World War is a childhood memory of Anderson shelters, blackout and rationing. As I grew up, I became aware of cities full of bomb sites, blooming with buddleia and willow herb. As I began to travel as a young adult, I found still worse scenes of destruction in the cities of Europe. Most recently of all, I saw Auschwitz.

We must remember these things, and the bitter loss of human life they represent, both to honour those who died and strengthen our resolve never to let them happen again.

Memories can be bitter, feeding hatred and revenge. Memories can also be healed, so as to become the necessary soil for purpose and hope. So we need to forgive, but not to forget.

The Right Reverend Alan Chesters MA
The Bishop of Blackburn

Although I was only seven years old and lived in a part of Britain which had few air raids, I well remember the remarkable sense of relief which came over my family and the West Yorkshire village in which we lived at that time. My own small part, along with the other children, was to help in building our bonfire and going to a celebration party.

At the time I had no idea what the armed forces had achieved or, indeed, of the deprivation under which we lived for, being young, I had no experiences of better times. I have increasingly come to realise just how close we came to losing our freedom and without that the opportunity to free the rest of Europe.

As one who has, in his ministry, had a particular concern

for the education of the young I believe it is important that each generation is reminded of the sacrifices made by so many in the hope that we shall all work together for peace among the Nations and for disputes to be settled by negotiation rather than by the use of arms.

The Right Reverend David Bonser
The Bishop of Bolton

During the Second World War I was only a small school boy. However, in our small avenue, there was a family who had a youngster near my own age – his father was captured early in the War and only returned at the end. The father of another family that we knew was killed.

On VE Day the whole avenue celebrated. There had been suffering and caring to a degree I have not known since and 'now' we could enjoy peace. My sharpest memory is of this event, but that celebration came out of the sadness: the neighbourliness out of suffering.

We do seem only to become fully considerate when we are 'up against it', and in the background to all this, men and women died and lost loved ones. Their lives must not be allowed to pass from our memory because it is only as we remember them that we are fully human with each other.

The Right Reverend Paul Barber MA
The Bishop of Brixworth

Around the age of seven in 1942, with my father away overseas, I became very conscious of the progress of the Second World War. I became an avid reader of newspapers and remember, through that medium and on the radio, D-Day and the Battle of Arnhem with special clarity.

Years later I visited the Oosterbecke War Graves Cemetery at Arnhem and was very moved as I walked among the hundreds and hundreds of grave stones commemorating youngsters of 18, 19 and 20 who had died there.

I remember one gravestone with this inscription: 'We prayed for you, Lennie, but we prayed in vain.'

As a one-time RBL Chaplain and now as a Bishop I have sometimes used that inscription as a starting point for sermons. I believe very deeply that Lennie, with countless others, did not die in vain. Nor were prayers for them ever wasted.

They played their part in overcoming a great evil, and we can only remember them with the utmost gratitude and respect.

The Right Reverend Martyn Jarrett
The Bishop of Burnley

I was born in 1944. My earliest memory is that of my father in his soldier's uniform. I grew up in a world heavy with memories of war. Bomb sites were my frequent playgrounds. Remembrance of that Second World War into which I was born, but of which I knew so little, has been part of my life. Across the newspaper headlines of my childhood came the names of such places as Korea, Cyprus, Malaya. In my adult life it has been such places as Northern Ireland, The Falklands, The Gulf. John Donne rightly said, 'No man is an island'. The suffering of the war impinges on our fellow human beings. It impinges on those who care. It impinges upon us.

Remembrancetide should underline the fact that human life is not cheap. Those long lines of war graves remind us that life is a gift, a gift which too many were denied enjoying to the full. Paradoxically, the wonder of life is appreciated most as we experience the loss of it. Life is worth having. That is what those who struggle to improve others' lives know. That others might have the gift of life is the great motivation that causes heroic people to lay it down on others' behalf. A true value placed on life and a determination that all should be able to enjoy such life as far as is possible, whether in Burnley, Belfast, Bosnia or Bangladesh, free from the horrors against which good men took up arms, would be a good legacy from all we call at Remembrancetide.

The Right Reverend Eric Waldram Kemp
The Bishop of Chichester

It is right and important that we should continue to remember the sacrifices of those who gave their lives in the two world wars. As well as expressing our thankfulness for what they did, it reminds us that peace will not be maintained without sacrifice, and, therefore, that we must all consider very carefully what sacrifices are needed of all of us and of all our rulers and statesmen if the rule of international law is to become really effective and the maintenance of international peace and order really to be secured.

The Right Reverend Michael E. Vickers
The Bishop of Colchester

In 1979 I spent a holiday in Crete with German and English friends. Two memories of that time live with me. One was the refusal of a guide to take our German friends to parts of the island where he was ready to take us. The other was going with one of our English friends to a cemetery searching for the grave of a colleague killed during one of the less publicised operations of the Second World War.

It not only opened a floodgate of wartime memories: it laid bare the unhealed wounds from which so long afterwards Europe is still suffering.

As a Chaplain myself for many years to a branch of the Royal Air Force Association I have had some opportunity to see such unhealed wounds in a number of personal contexts.

Memories that linger hurtfully must be used positively to avoid a repetition of what we passed through 50 years ago.

The Right Reverend Simon Barrington-Ward
The Bishop of Coventry

In the summer of 1940 I was at school in Dunchurch near Rugby and my parents decided to withdraw me before the end of term, telling me that they wanted me to be with

133

them at that time. I understood later that my father who, as a journalist, was well informed, felt that an invasion of Britain was imminent and that we should be together as a family when it came. In that same school I remember sitting in the Headmaster's Study listening to Churchill pledging that 'We would fight on the beaches . . . ...' and that 'We would never surrender . . . ..' I will never forget the impact on us youngsters of the Battle of Britain, of the bombing of Coventry 14 miles away, nor of the news of those early turning points, Stalingrad and El Alamein, nor of the gradual liberation of Europe with all its cost in lives and suffering which some have borne to this day.

I rejoice that today children and young people can enter into something of that experience, when they come through the Ruins of the Cathedral at Coventry into the new part, with its vision of the hope of peace, or when I see many of the descendants of those who gave their lives for our freedom, thronging round at our Thanksgiving Service on Remembrance Day in the Memorial Park.

We must deeply and gratefully remember those who stood in the breach for us if we are to 're-member', to bring together into one, humanity across the world today. Only as we truly recall the past can we hope and pray to change the future for us all. That is the message of the Cross of Nails in the heart of Coventry Cathedral which summons new generations, as we recall with deep thankfulness the sacrifices made in war in the past for us, to sacrifice ourselves in turn to seek by God's grace to raise up a just and peaceful world for the future.

The Right Reverend Dr Wilfred Wood
The Bishop of Croydon

Many of those who died in the Second World War gave their lives as their way of saying "no" to the kind of world they did not want.

Almighty God in His wisdom, created a world of many peoples, nationalities and ethnic groups and revealed himself by becoming the son of a Jewish woman. He taught that human beings should love their neighbours as themselves and that all human beings, irrespective of national or ethnic origin, are neighbours.

But in our lifetime a small group of men had other ideas and set out to re-order the world, to ensure the permanent superiority of their own nation and ethnic group. Nazi concentration camps, gas ovens, surgical experiments marked new depths of man's inhumanity to man. Their designs were defeated but at the cost of millions of lives. British lives, Russian lives, African, Asian and other lives: Christians, Jews, Sikhs, Moslems, Hindus, Communists and adherents of other faiths were among the dead. Black men and women, white and brown, all laid down their lives to prevent a fascist and racist domination of the world, and to preserve freedom as they knew and loved it.

In biblical usage the word 'remembrance' has a particular meaning. To remember something is to make it once more active in our lives – for good or ill. Remembrance is a form of life – not to be remembered is non-existence, and in the Old Testament hell is sometimes referred to as the land of non-remembrance. It is right that we remember.

Today if our remembrance of those who stood shoulder to shoulder and fell alongside each other in the struggle against Facism is to mean anything, it must include a determination that such costly sacrifices must not be demanded again. Wherever racist bigotry rears its head, whether in the crude slogans of trouble-makers at football matches or in the polished accents of some politicians, people of decency and goodwill must speak up against it to ensure that it gains no ground in our political processes or support from our young people. We must remember the glorious dead when in our time we live by and keep alive, the ideals for which they died – ideals of freedom, faith, justice and human dignity.

The Right Reverend Peter Dawes
The Bishop of Derby

I can recollect, as if it was yesterday, the room in our house where we gathered round the radio to hear Neville Chamberlain conclude 'This country is therefore at war with Germany'. I was eleven years old. I remember five minutes later finding my mother crying bitterly in the kitchen. My father had served almost entirely throughout the First World War in France in the Royal Artillery. Fifteen minutes after that, the air raid sirens with their eerie, warbling sound began. We huddled together in a corner of the room with our gas masks until, a few minutes later – it being a false alarm – the all-clear sounded.

Living in Bromley in Kent, meant that for parts of the War one was certainly in the front line of action. The raids became more real during and following the Battle of Britain, and then, towards the end of the War, came the V1s, the flying bombs, an amazing sight at night with the flames pouring out of their engines, and the V2s.

War itself, as I know from personal experience is evil, grim and horrible but it is important to remember and honour those who risked their lives and those who were wounded or died in the World Wars. There is a story in the Old Testament where three of David's friends undertake a very risky adventure, just to bring him a drink of water. When they bring it back, David won't drink it, but pours it on the ground, saying that it is not water but blood of the men who had risked their lives. It was, therefore, too precious to drink. The costs in lives and misery have been too great for future generations to waste the opportunities for peace in Europe and elsewhere.

The Right Reverend Richard Llewellin
The Bishop of Dover

I was born in South Wales just before the Second World War, but my childhood was spent in India, and my family did not return to the United Kingdom until the War was over. However, my journeys in the Diocese of Canterbury often remind me of what was happening in this country during those years. Here and there I see the ruins of ancient churches destroyed in the Blitz and never re-built. Their loss was one part of the huge price paid by millions of our fellow countrymen to preserve for us the freedom to worship without fear.

We do need to be reminded of that cost. Remembering is one way of renewing our determination to oppose injustice and oppression wherever we find it. The memory of what past generations have done for us can spur us to greater efforts in our service of the generations to come.

The Right Reverend Rupert (and Gesine) Hoare
The Bishop of Dudley and his wife

My wife comes from Germany; I am from Britain. We married in Germany in 1965 and from the very beginning of our marriage we have been committed to the process of reconciliation within Europe. We both consider this absolutely vital, both on the political and on the religious levels. We do not believe that the full effects of either the First or the Second World Wars have yet been overcome by us Europeans. There is lots yet to do.

At the time of the Second World War we were both small children in Germany and England respectively. We experienced the war largely through the eyes and ears of our parents. We have discovered that our respective fathers were both in France at the same time towards the beginning of the war on different sides of the conflict.

Over the years we have heard a great deal about the suffering endured on both sides in that awful conflict of the Second World War and we are committed to seeing that National Socialism never rears its head again as a force within Europe. We both of us honour and respect those who stood against the National Socialists in the forces of the Allies, and those within Germany who did all they could to resist that wicked and tyrannical regime. We remember them with respect and gratitude.

The Right Reverend Michael Turnbull
Bishop of Durham

I confess to sometimes having irreverent thoughts during the silence on Remembrance Day. I glance around wondering "What are all these people thinking about?". After all an increasing number have no recollection of the people and events we are seeking to remember.

For some, of course, remembrance will be a solemn

calling to mind of deeply sad and harrowing experiences. It will be bringing into focus the images of comrades who didn't live to remember. They will be remembered as jolly and fearful friends, as ordinary soldiers who became lasting heros, as fathers and sons who left behind families permanently scarred.

For others, without those intensely personal memories, the silence will be a recollection of the price which unknown warriors paid for the freedoms we now enjoy. There will be an element of anger and wonder that so much had to be given to reverse the follies of mankind. There will be steely resolution that what those sacrifices won will never be wasted or thrown away.

But, for an increasing number, remembrance will be the bridge between what is history and the present which shapes the future. Now is only a blink in the silence as the eyes of the mind turn to what lies ahead.

Jesus of Nazareth, on the night before he died that others might live, left his own act of remembrance. For those present at the Last Supper it was a harrowing mixture of memories and fearfulness of the future. For the generations which have followed, the solemn remembrance, in the ordinary things of bread and wine, have been a sign of hope that sacrificial death achieves a promise for the future.

For all of us, collectively, remembrance will include reminiscence, recollection and resolution. Without each of these elements the Act of Remembrance can have no justification, as I furtively glance around in the silence, I know they are there.

The Right Reverend Stephen Sykes
The Bishop of Ely

As a person born in 1939 my knowledge of the events of the Second World War is derived from reading. But that reading has fully convinced me of the continuing importance of those events even fifty years later.

I have become conscious of the terrifying power of racist ideologies to destroy and devastate whole communities. As one considers the contemporary fate of so many of the countries of Europe and the Far East which were subject to aggression and invasion, it seems to me that we are still living in the aftermath of that war.

In my view it is important that we remember those events and those who gave their lives, before God. Then we are obliged to try and see the truth as He sees it; to rejoice in courage, but to admit failure; to be glad that freedom triumphed, but to be ready to forgive. Above all remembrance should be an act of commitment to the highest values to which humanity can together aspire.

The Right Reverend John Klyberg
The Bishop of Fulham

The value of observing Remembrance Day is increasingly questioned in some circles. It is said to be meaningless for the majority of people who were either not born at the time of the Second World War or who were too young for the services.

I believe such a view to be mistaken. We are all indebted to those who, in the past, have tried to make the world a better place. Christians are indebted to Jesus on the cross – the fact that we were not there at the time is irrelevant. It is the consequences that we are thankful for. Likewise, we should welcome the opportunity of honouring those who gave their lives so that this island would remain free.

The Right Reverend Michael Adie
The Bishop of Guildford

On the day that war was declared in 1939 I was a small boy carrying home a precious bowl of goldfish which I had just bought at Woolworths. The goldfish were the first war casualties that I knew because I had to leave them and was bundled off into the country for safe keeping. As the war continued I recognised as an early lesson that goldfish were nothing to the increasing horror and destruction that nations and people were inflicting on one another. The devastation, the tragedy and the hatred have taken years to reconstruct and heal. From time to time since the end of the War we have heard the phrase 'The cost of living'. This is normally taken to refer to our material standards of wealth and possessions. It ought to be a continuing reminder of the price paid by people during a war whose memories still live on. Those who do not have direct memory of war none the less need to remember the cost of living.

The Right Reverend William Roe
The Bishop of Huntingdon

The day war broke out we stood in our front room, my mother put her arm around my shoulders and said "The world will never be the same again." Nor was it. My wife's father came home from Dunkirk by dead of night. Next morning when she went into the bathroom, there was water in the bath coloured deep red with blood. "Don't worry darling," said my future mother-in-law, "it isn't Daddy's blood." That seemed to make matters worse.

We had airmen billeted on us while they finished their basic training. I used to like standing in the garden with them while they cleaned their kit. One day a wiry little Scotsman from the Shetlands thrust his bayonet into the earth to clean it. As he withdrew it, he looked at it and was suddenly violently sick.

For us children, those were the days of 'goodies' and 'baddies'. The baddies wore coal scuttle helmets and were surrounded by darkness. We were the goodies. It seemed that we were inspired by fighting for a common cause. Evil was always 'out there.' What I didn't realise was the devastating effect of death and maiming on countless families.

Evil is still 'out there' and within us, but I hope that now we are beginning to learn that war does not overcome it. Those war memorials itemise the cost of learning that lesson, which must never be forgotten.

The Right Reverend John Hughes
The Bishop of Kensington

There is one person who in his life and death still sums up for me the Second World War, and the more so as the years go by. Alan was the fiance of a younger friend of my mother, who had for the duration of the war returned to her old job in the works account office at GKN Darlaston. He was a qualified draughtsman who had good career prospects in a place like the Black Country, in those days a thriving hub of the War Effort.

As children we loved his visits. He could draw aircraft with great accuracy and we shared his delight when he was accepted for training as a pilot in the Royal Air Force. Even greater was his delight on being posted to a Lancaster Squadron. On his leave we got him involved in a game of backyard cricket. A lot of friends as well as the grown ups where all drawn in and there developed a heady and exciting joy not unmixed with the pride we all felt in being close to one who was for such as us a hero. Nobody was to know that his cheery goodbye would be the last.

A week later he failed to return from his first mission, one of the big Lancaster raids. For a long time we believed he would be found safe and well. Our friends who had only met him once would ask how is Alan, such was the impression he made, not by bravado but the gentle good homour of a lovely man. Each Remembrance Sunday I remember his soul. He was very special to us and yet was so normal. It was the sacrifice of many like him, normally gentle good people, who gave their all and ensured the survival of our country. They were remembered by children and friends they played with in the homes and streets of the land they loved. They are still remembered.

The Right Reverend Martin Wharton
The Bishop of Kingston

Although I was born towards the end of the Second World War, I cannot remember it. I recall stories told to me by my father about his service in the Royal Navy and about the bombing of the northern shipbuilding town where I grew up. But the Second World War, like the First, is something I have only heard about from others and read about with horror and fascination.

In the course of my life, I have come to know many women and men who showed astonishing bravery and endurance during those years. I am very aware of the countless people who gave their lives for their country in the face of unutterable horror and brutality. Their sacrifices must never be forgotten, but that does not mean there is any glory to be found in war. For all the people, the stories, the books and the films which tell of heroic effort and brave sacrifice, the truth is that war is a terrible, terrible business.

In parish churches up and down this land, there are memorials to those who gave up their lives in the fight against evil. These are the memorials to all those young lives, given, for our freedom. We need to remember them. We need to remember the courage and the carnage, the horror and the heroism. We need to remember in a way that does justice to God who calls us to a quality of human relationships, which transcend all national and regional frontiers (and which the Bible calls eternal.) Above all we need to remember so that we can renew our commitment to work for reconciliation and peace in the present and future.

The Right Reverend Malcolm Menin
The Bishop of Knaresborough

I was almost seven when war was declared. I can remember the sense of foreboding that was around, and I remember being the first in my family to have a gas mask. It all seemed both exciting and very frightening. As the tide turned in North Africa and the build-up towards D-Day took place, my school friends and I were busy making model tanks and planes.

Only five years after the end of the war I was myself a soldier in the Fourth Hussars, in tanks, just for two years at the time of the Korean War. I met and worked with many who had fought and had a sense of being part of something very good, successful and victorious.

Since those days I have spent many holidays in France and Italy: I have sometimes stopped and walked round the war cemeteries. It has made me acutely aware of the horrific cost of war, and its futility. I am not a pacifist, because I am aware that Facism was a great evil, and evil has to be resisted, if necessary at the risk of one's life. I am increasingly aware, as current smaller conflicts rage around the world, of the disorder at the heart of humanity, which produces such awful slaughter and suffering.

I have come to the conclusion that nuclear war is something which risks not just the lives of hosts of people but the future of the whole created order as we know it, and that to prepare to wage such a war is too great an evil to contemplate. I therefore joined CND as a matter of conscience several years ago.

The Right Reverend Keith Sutton
The Bishop of Lichfield

One night during the Second World War, my uncle took me to the brow of a hill behind our cottage in the Surrey countryside. He showed me a great red glow in the sky. It was London burning after an air attack. I was 10 years old.

That red glow filled me with a sense of the immense power of evil in the world. That is why I will always honour those who resisted that evil by laying down their lives. That is why the 'Golden Book of Remembrance' is so important. By remembering the sacrifices of the past, we are better able to resist the evils of the future.

The Right Reverend Robert Maynard Hardy
The Bishop of Lincoln

My family suffered remarkably little from the effects of the Second World War. My father was in a reserve occupation, and we were not much troubled by air raids or bombing. So although I was aware of friends' fathers who were away on active service, my own memories are ones of excitement rather than alarm: having a real soldier billetted on us, clambering over a tank, sitting in a Spitfire during various War Weapons' Weeks.

What I do remember, particularly clearly, however, was the sense of looking forward to 'When the war was over', the feeling of idealism, and the will to make the world (even my small part of it) a better place. We need, I believe, to recover that feeling now, and 'remembrance' of the cost, and the sacrifice of so many is a critical and essential part of this. It brings both healing and inspiration.

W.H. Auden, after the Second World War, in two lines which he called 'Epitaph for the Unknown Soldier' expressed this perfectly:

To save your world, you asked this man to die,
Would this man, could he see you now, ask why.

Those are sentiments which my generation and those who follow us, would do well to ponder.

The Right Reverend David Michael Hope
The Bishop of London

My earliest remembrances of the Second World War are of a three wheeler tandem, which my twin sister and I shared, and gas masks. The tandem once became stuck between the blast wall and the actual door of the air raid shelter as we attempted, along with other people and things, to make sure that our most prized possessions should also be safe from any bombing.

Already though, on family occasions, my father and grandmother reminiscing about the old times would tell of how my father's elder brother had gone off to the trenches of the First World War never to be heard of again. They were very moving stories and became part of the family, its life and its tradition.

There were many sacrifices to be made – the supreme sacrifice of human life given up so that we may live in peace and freedom. There were the smaller and lesser sacrifices too which people made in families and streets and neighbourhoods, to support and encourage and help each other in times of need. Such sacrificial living must continue as a sign of a fully mature and civilised people and nation.

The Right Reverend David Sheppard
The Bishop of Liverpool

Remembrance of the Second World War brings deep thankfulness to my mind. As a teenager during the war, I saw and felt the cost mainly through the eyes of adults – my mother's tears at the declaration of war in 1939 and her words, "I remember the last one". She had been widowed before the 1939 War: we were especially glad at her deepening friendship with a Polish Airman: and felt the pain when we received the letter saying he was missing, believed killed.

It is important that we sharpen those feelings which can be blunted by the passing of years, so that we think again about the cost of violence and war, and see the dangers of nationalistic fears and ambitions. Television brings home to us how brutal civil wars can be. While we thank God for peace in our part of the world for 50 years, we remember that the world has seen 20 million people killed in wars during those years, leaving 15 million refugees.

Tolerance should be very high in the creed of Christians. The New Testament speaks of God's purpose to break down the barriers of enmity and prejudice between nations, between Ethnic Groups, between families and between individuals. He has made that possible, I believe, through the costly self giving of his Son Jesus Christ: His purpose is to create a single new humanity.

Remembrance of war reminds us of how difficult that is. Fears, prejudices, old bitter memories, can destroy co-operative and trusting partnerships between nations and groups. And the challenge to be peace makers comes to us as individuals as well as to nations.

The Right Reverend Gavin Reid
The Bishop of Maidstone

As with many families, the war brought disruption and separation for me. After very heavy bombing of my home town of Greenock, I was sent away to live with relatives for over a year. My time away from the rest of my family, however, was nothing compared with the longer separations that many of my contemporaries had to endure.

I remember clearly one Christmas when the family was together and my brother and I went out for a walk with my father. It was at a time when things were going badly for the allies on the battle front. My brother asked my father: "Are we really going to win this war?" My father's reply was immediate: "of course we are". I don't think for one moment, he was putting on a brave front or simply trying to reassure an anxious child. His reply revealed the spirit that was in the nation as a whole. We simply knew that we were in the right and that our cause would prevail. When a nation feels like that, anything is possible.

Sadly, in peace, the British nation has not been able to discover such a unifying sense of purpose. As we look back on those tragic and yet triumphant days, my prayer is that we might be made to reflect on the fact that we were fighting for far more than survival. We had a vision of what was right and we were not prepared to settle for anything less.

As we face the future in an uncertain world with differing threats to those of 1939, we need to discover a new vision that will again lift us beyond selfish and narrow, personal or nationalistic concerns.

The Right Reverend P.J. Firth
The Bishop of Malmesbury

My personal war memorial is based on three memories. I remember a school friend leaving to join the Black Watch in 1941. He came to say goodbye to my parents, resplendent in full officer's uniform. Three months later, we heard he had died in Burma. I was twelve at the time, and the loss was incomprehensible. I remember stopping to look at a wayside stone along the desolate road which runs through the mountains of Southern Italy – the Gran Sasso – and realising that it commemorated the death of a twenty-one-year-old New Zealander, killed there in 1944; and wondering how he viewed the thought of dying twelve thousand miles from home in a conflict he can barely have understood. And I remember camping with my family on a lonely Turkish beach, and being told by a passing doctor – who had seen our camp fire – that this was Gallipoli, where my father had landed in 1916. We visited the huge memorial to his, and other, regiments the next day.

These three memories are far clearer than all the bombs and doodlebugs, gas masks and visiting Americans of my childhood. They symbolise the terminal demands we make of others when we lack vigilance and understanding of the world outside our town or country. They are a constant reminder for the need to be responsible for our democracy, our freedoms, our neighbours here, in Germany, in Bosnia and Beirut, in Northern Ireland or South Africa.

War is the final breakdown of communication and understanding between the few, which results in the deaths of the many. There is a continuing need to be reminded of those sacrifices, so that we do not demand them of our children and grandchildren.

The Right Reverend Christopher Mayfield
The Bishop of Manchester

I was born at the end of 1935. So I am one of the many fortunate children who lived through the Second World War but whose life was almost entirely unaffected by it. My father served in the Royal Navy, helping to lay anti-submarine nets at the entrances of African ports; and an uncle served in the army; parachuting into France; thankfully both men returned safely to our family in 1945. Cousins and friends were evacuated from London and Bristol to stay with us in Worcester. But I was able to live in my own home undisturbed. Bombs rained on nearby Birmingham; as a precaution we filled the bath with water every night; while a fleeing German bomber off-loaded his weapons to our house which blew out our windows, little other damage was done. Food and clothing were rationed; but my mother ensured that we were never hungry or unclothed. My schooling was uninterrupted. We were indeed most fortunate.

However the news (newspapers and radio only in those days) and later films and books made me realise that others had not been so lucky. Four years peace time service in the Royal Air Force in the late 1950s brought home to me the continuing presence of violence and war in every part of the world throughout the years since the end of the Second World War. My continuing ministry as a Priest and a Bishop brings me into regular contact with people who still suffer in account of war. Some are those who mourn the loss of members of their families; others are women in their 70s whose boyfriends and sweethearts served in the Armed Forces but never came back; and others ex-servicemen and women who not only lost comrades and friends, but also lost health, limbs, and well-being. Damaged buildings can be replaced, bombed cities can be re-built and re-newed; but human lives cannot be replaced or restored. In war there are no winners, only degrees of loss. Courage and heroism take second place to sacrifice and grief.

I believe that those of us who are fortunate enough to be alive today are under an obligation to remember with thankfulness all those who won our freedom from potential enslavement. We need to think sombrely about how we use our freedom and our gifts – so that we can all contribute to the establishing of peace and justice in England, Europe, and throughout the world.

The Right Reverend Stephen Venner
The Bishop of Middleton

A recent report by a Teacher's Union highlighted the growing problem of young children actively choosing to watch violent and sadistic videos. It reported that many children, even of infant school age, rejoice in recounting the hideous scenes they have witnessed. What frightened me was the report's statement that for these children there was no moral dimension to the videos – it did not occur to them that violence, pain and the abuse of others might be wrong or evil!

To remember is to bring the past into the present. Those who have lived through and experienced the horrors of war need to remember and to help children and grand-children to understand. Peace is not the absence of war but a determination to treat ones fellows with respect, dignity and justice. Peace is God's will for his world, for only in peace can all people grow into fullness and happiness.

To achieve peace is costly. To maintain peace is costly. It is my prayer that today's children will all learn that the price is worth paying.

The Right Reverend Andrew Alexander Graham
The Bishop of Newcastle

Throughout the Second World War I was a schoolboy in Kent and can remember vividly the day on which war broke out; the great formations of German planes which repeatedly made their way over our garden towards London during the following year; the Battle of Britain fought in cloudless skies; and the trophies in the form of bullets and shrapnel found in the garden.

I have many other vivid recollections of those five years: for instance, the day of my confirmation was the first day on which flying bombs came over South East England, and this added to the excitement of the occasion. Also I remember the immense sense of relief on V.E. Day when the whole town seemed to go wild and school discipline broke down.

In retrospect I am astonished at the outward calm and confidence of my parents and schoolteachers. They must have known what close run things were both the Battle of Britain and the Battle of the Atlantic, but they never showed any sense of anxiety to us who were children. Perhaps they had an inbred British confidence that disaster would be averted.

As after 50 years I look back on the momentous events which were taking place during my childhood, we can see a strange mixture of Grief and Glory. There was much that was noble and idealistic, much heroism, valour and selflessness; there was the Glory. Equally there was the Grief of knowing about the brutality, pain and destructive violence which are an inevitable result of warfare. In retrospect, the category of Tragedy seems appropriate, for in any Tragedy, Grief and Glory are to be found. The Glory and the Grief correspond to the grandeur and misery of man, about which Blaise Pascal wrote so movingly in the 17th century. The misery of man led him to seek God, and Christian faith is rooted, characteristically, in Tragedy, for on Golgotha will be found both Grief and Glory in equal measure. The remembrance of that event helps us to interpret and to understand the events of fifty years ago which we particularly remember this year.

The Right Reverend Peter Nott
The Bishop of Norwich

What sort of remembering will there be this year? Our national remembrance this year will be marked in churches up and down the land by thanksgiving to God, by celebrations and by compassion for those still affected by the suffering of warfare through bereavement or injury. For those who lived through the war, personal experiences will naturally be relived with renewed vividness. I was a child through the war years, and my memories are now vague, but a few are so clear they will live with me always.

My family were living in Plymouth at the beginning of the war, and we were there during the heavy bombing which devastated the city. I was only 7 years old at the time, but my memories are still vivid. Small boys at that time collected souvenirs the morning after raids, pieces of shrapnel from bombs or anti aircraft shells and, if you could find one, the tail fin of an incendiary bomb was highly prized. We had little idea of what all the destruction meant, and small boys do not talk to one another much about their fears. But we were afraid, terribly afraid, and the memories of sitting under the stairs wakeful through the night are all too real – the stomach-turning wailing of the siren followed often by silence, and ears straining for the first sounds of the bombers – then the terrifying noise, the whistle of bombs, gauging how near the bomb would fall and waiting for the awful explosion that would follow.

When we remember war, it is dangerously easy to forget the non-combatants, especially women and children, who suffered through warfare, who were injured, bereaved, and killed in their thousands. It is dangerously easy to talk in wrong ways about those who died in war – language about our glorious dead can easily lead to a glorifying of war itself. No one who has experienced an air raid is in danger of thinking that warfare is anything but terrible.

When people, mostly men, remember war, they often talk about the positive as well as the negative aspects of their experience. Of course they were frightened too, they lost friends who were killed, they suffered physical and mental injuries which sometimes crippled them for life. But they can also remember positive things – examples of great courage, dogged endurance and good companionship. That kind of remembering is good as well as remembering the horrors of war, because through it one can learn how sometimes good can come from evil, and it can provide us with lessons for the future.

But what about those who were non-combatants, especially the women and children of the air raids? Is there anything positive for us to remember – any lesson or example for us to pass on to our children and grandchildren?

There is one great meaning I think, in all that pain. I did not realise it at the time, but the lesson was taught to me one sunny morning in Plymouth I think perhaps a year before the terrible air raids. I was walking with my father and looking up we saw fighters high in the sky engaged in a battle. They were too far away to hear anything, but soon one plane was hit and dived down in flames. It soon became clear it was a German aircraft, and I cheered loudly, jumping up and down in patriotic excitement.

"Don't cheer" my father said, "Remember that was probably someone's Daddy too."

The lesson is this. There is a fellowship of suffering, a fellowship which knows no boundary of nation or race or religion. We in England also shared a fellowship of suffering with the women and children of Dresden, Cologne, Hamburg and Berlin. They were someone's mothers' to; someone's grandparents, someone's children who suffered and died.

Suffering knows no boundaries, and we should value that fellowship still today. It should enable us to sympathise, to be at one with all the innocents who suffer throughout the world, in Northern Ireland, in the Middle

East, in Africa and Latin America. With all these people we are most truly at one.

Suffering is always a dark mystery, and tragedy is no less tragic if you are a Christian. But we believe in hope because of Easter, the time when the church reaffirms its faith in the God who can bring light out of darkness, and joy out of tragedy; the God in whom there is hope, always hope, because in Christ no one and nothing is lost for ever.

The Right Reverend Richard Harries
The Bishop of Oxford

To be human is to remember. Memories are an essential part of each one of us. No less significantly they are a crucial part of our national identity. It is important that we remember the great events of the past as a nation, for these help to shape and direct us. That is why, although the Second World War is not remembered personally by many millions now, it has always seemed to me important to remember it publicly on Remembrance Sunday.

Shortly after the outbreak of the Second World War my father was posted to Washington, to buy signals equipment for the British Army. My mother, sister and I followed shortly afterwards. We went in a large convoy, on a ship that had been requisitioned from carrying a cargo of oranges I remember! Whereas one of the great Queen's can cross the Atlantic in five days, we took nearly a month. We had to dodge the U Boats and so our route took us nearly up to Iceland and Greenland. Fortunately I was too young to be scared but we had to wear life jackets all the time and my mother told me that she was terrified.

We came back from America in time for some flying bombs and scuttling under the stairs. But for most of the war I was in America and American support during the Second World War has meant that I have not shared the anti-American bias that has characterized so many parts of the world during the last two decades.

Sadly, in a world characterized by ruthless violence, it is still necessary for nations to collaborate to uphold basic human values. I believe that it was right that we resisted the Nazis by force, in the uncertain times in which we now live,

I hope and pray that diplomacy and international organs like the United Nations will be able to be decisive enough at times of crisis, so that we can avoid war on such scale again.

The Right Reverend William Westwood
The Bishop of Peterborough

Every time I visit a village church in my diocese I look at the Memorials to two World Wars and I recollect that those whose names I read there were no more than boys when they died.

It is always the young we ask to surrender their youth for us in time of war.

My father served in the Great War – all four years of it – and I served at the end of the World War. Praise God, my son in his thirties has never had to face this possibility and pray God that my grandson, aged 2, may never have to do it.

I remember that it is always the young that we ask and I am sad.

The Right Reverend John Finney
The Bishop of Pontefract

As a boy growing up into my teens during the Second World War I have a kaleidoscope of memories – scrabbling for pieces of shrapnel and parachute cord with others from my school . . . . being evacuated from my home . . . . spending long nights in the shelter listening to the drone of German bombers . . . . being excited by the radio news of the D-Day landings . . . . being in London swept along by the crowds during the VJ celebrations. It was a mixture of fear and elation, bewilderment and uncertainty.

However the abiding memory is of the news of friends being killed or coming back maimed. These were mainly the sixth form heroes on the sports field who became no more than an inscribed name on a war memorial. It reminds us that war may have it's fellowship and it's glamour but at heart it is brutal, costly and evil. We must do all we can to pray and work towards peace in a very troubled and divided world and in particular to seek that harmony of spirit in the heart of all people which means that they are not swept away by false nationalisms or contempt for other peoples. The world has barely learnt the full meaning of Christ's words to love our friends, let alone his command to love our enemies.

The Right Reverend Peter St. G. Vaughan
The Bishop of Ramsbury

I was a schoolboy during the Second World War. Two poignant memories of 1940 come to mind. The first is when all women and children had to evacuate from the South coast over the Dunkirk weekend. I remember standing on the station at Swindon, with my football in my hand, and my mother desperately trying to find out from the train drivers where the trains were going as we were on our way to Cheltenham. All over the platforms lay the exhausted soldiers who had been evacuated from France. I remember the courage with which my mother faced that journey as she was pregnant and feeling very unwell.

The second memory is of a severe air raid on Cheltenham in December of that year. We spent the whole night in one room with all the other occupants of a large house of flats. We were drilled how to crouch each time we heard the whistling of the bombs. The next morning I heard that my school had been hit and the classrooms destroyed. As a pupil at Dean Close Junior School, the following term we had to have our classes in the Senior school.

Somehow, even though a boy, one can remember that these experiences brought out the best in people. The leadership of our country at the time never let us feel that we could lose the war.

The Right Reverend Timothy Bavin
The Bishop of Portsmouth

One of the most vivid of my childhood memories is of being taken from my bed and tucked up, together with my small sister, in blankets under the kitchen table, whilst my parents sat drinking tea by the Aga.

We were living in Buckinghamshire and although I can recall the sound of the doodlebugs (and that awful silence between the cutting out of their engine and their detonation), I remember only one bomb which rocked the house as it exploded a few fields away.

Later, at school in Windsor, we regularly retreated to the cellars when the air raid warning sounded. I don't think we minded our lessons being disrupted, but the sound of that siren today (in recordings or, occasionally, live) sends a chill down my spine still.

For the uncertainty of war adds to its horror and it seems so inappropriate and irresponsible for civilised peoples to seek to settle their disputes by violence, especially when it is indiscriminate in its victims and on so massive a scale. Moreover, it is sad that it takes a war to unite a nation and to bring out the best qualities of courage, co-operation, self-sacrifice and good humour in its citizens.

The Right Reverend David N. de L. Young
The Bishop of Ripon

I was a boy during the Second World War, aged 13 when it finished. I remember the celebrations, travelling to London with my family on V.E. Day. I remember the sense of thanksgiving and relief. Like many other families my own family knew loss. I had one cousin killed, another was a prisoner of war with the Japanese. Most families experienced loss and grief at this time.

I belong to a generation which was brought up to believe that wars should be fought only for high ideals, and reflection has not altered that view. Wars are brutal, tragic, but sometimes necessary, however costly they may be. Remembrance Day is a reminder of the cost borne by a whole society, but especially by families whose members have been killed, captured, wounded or harmed in some way.

As one who has never fought in a war, I recognise that cost. Remembrance is a personal reminder to me of what I owe to others.

The Right Reverend Graham James
The Bishop of St Germans

I was not even born when the Second World War ended. Yet I represent a generation which owes its liberties to the sacrifices made by the many who fought in the cause of freedom.

Whenever I have conducted a service of remembrance and ex-combatants have been present, I have been conscious that they have been recalling friends who fell, neighbours who were maimed, and companions who comforted them. Written on some faces is the legacy of experiences which can never be named. It's the tragedy of war which drives some Christians into pacifism, and I am sure that we need their witness. But war is not always the product of imperialism or thoughtless patriotism. Just as frequently it results from our sense of justice and desire to see right prevail. That's why the Second World War doesn't seem ultimately to be a matter simply of regret, despite the bungles, the blanket and the blitz.

I don't believe the passage of years means that we should forget to offer thanksgiving for the freedoms won by those who died. The very word 'remember' means that we connect up our memories, and put things together to understand their significance. It's the very opposite of dismembering.

We don't mark the fiftieth anniversary of the end of the Second World War simply to honour the dead, though that is vital. We do so for the sake of our country's moral and spiritual health. For we will surely dismember if we do not remember.

The Right Reverend John Kirkham
The Bishop of Sherborne – Bishop to Her Majesty's Forces

I was a small boy when war broke out and I have vivid memories of the years that followed. We were living in a country village not far from Southampton and daily the war was being fought in the skies above us and felt in the villages and towns around us. I have memories of the night that Southampton went up in flames and the night sky ablaze while the air was full of the sound of exploding bombs: wave after wave of German planes flying daily over our rectory on bombing missions to the industrial midlands and the north: dog fights in the sky above us where the Battle of Britain was being fought: night after night villagers coming to our house as they sought refuge in our cellars. I remember, too, the woods and fields filled with military vehicles and personnel who had joined us from different parts of the world to take part in the invasion of Normandy.

In this special year we commemorate those events of fifty years ago and recall with gratitude the sacrifice of those who gave their lives. May the past and that for which they were fighting never be forgotten but remain an inspiration to others to build a better world. In my work as Bishop to Her Majesty's Armed Forces I travel extensively and wherever I go I am greatly impressed by the integrity and professionalism of our Armed Services. They demand our respect and support in the role which they are playing in creating and preserving peace. Peace should never be a time of relaxation between wars or a time for that self-interest and self-indulgence which afflicts our society today but it should be a time when people and nations look forward and work tirelessly for the creation of a better world in which war will be no more and where all God's children can live as brothers and sisters. Winston Churchill said "A nation which has forgotten its past can have no future". Those who fought and died fifty years ago in France, Burma, Italy and elsewhere were defending those great values on which our western civilisation is based and which were in danger of being lost – the value of the individual, freedom, justice, truth and kindness. A new day will never dawn with a new world order if we forget the past and those values for which so many fought and died. Traditional values and traditional beliefs matter. Peace has its perils no less than war and peace which neglects its spiritual values is the most perilous of all. A nation which becomes a spiritually lazy nation can quickly lose its vision, ignore its purpose and neglect its values and ideals while beginning to shake in its very foundations. By remembering the past and respecting that for which so many died we shall be safeguarding those values and ideals while assisting God in the creation of a better world with a future of peace and freedom.

The Right Reverend John Davies
The Bishop of Shrewsbury

I served in the Royal Air Force for some years, commencing at the very end of the 1939-45 war. One of my memories is the very wide variety of attitudes towards the whole notion of remembrance, which were expressed by my colleagues. Some of us were old, and had seen many years of service; others, like myself, were recruited right at the end of the war. I was deeply impressed by those who, while not objecting to the observance of remembrance, were careful to control their enthusiasm. This was partly because they recognised that the war had brought the deaths of vast numbers of people on both sides of the conflict, and that there was a real solidarity in death right across the political divisions; but a perhaps more common reason was that they were conscious that some memories were quite close enough to the surface without needing to be encouraged by an official programme. And there remain, I know, many people who experienced the horrors of war who want to keep entirely quiet during the annual commemoration in November. I say this, not to discourage the notion of remembrance, but to stress the need to be sensitive to those whose memory is very deeply scarred and for whom the public celebrations are extremely painful. They also are a part of our community.

The Right Reverend Noel Debroy Jones
The Bishop of Sodor and Man

In 1962 I joined the Royal Navy as a Chaplain, and in the following 27 years of service I had considerable contact with many different countries. Almost everywhere I experienced a hatred of war, and a determination to observe some form of Remembrances of sacrifices made by those who died in wars, so that lessons could be learned by later generations.

There is no dramatic way of doing this than by visiting War Graves around the globe and realising just how terrible has been the price of peace. The Graves, which are immaculately main-tained, declare at a glance the huge numbers of young men and women who have given their lives and who have met untimely ends.

My abiding memory will be of the 500 neat white crosses in a plot overlooking the blue waters surrounding the island of Labuan. Here, lying together, are Australians, Malays, Chinese, Indian and British personnel. Their names, ages, and country of origin are noted on the crosses in their serried ranks. There are some, which bear the statement, 'Known Only to God'. This simple wording speaks volumes. If God knows and cares for each and every one, how dare we forget?

The Right Reverend Noel Debroy Jones, The Lord Bishop of Sodor and Man, during his 27 years as a Royal Navy chaplain.
(Photo courtersy
The Lord Bishop of Sodor and Man)

The Right Reverend Roy Williamson
The Bishop of Southwark

Memory and hope are intimately connected. It is said that we live in days when there is a depreciation of memory and a ridicule of hope. The present, apparently, is all that matters. Perhaps that is why our age seems to have lost its way.

I have a vivid memory of the first air-raid over Belfast, my home city. As a boy of eight I recall taking refuge in the street shelter just outside our house. We lived in the shadow of the Belfast Shipyards and the bombs that fell on our street and on my school were clearly meant for a more significant target.

In my childish innocence and lack of perception there was a touch of glamour and excitement about the experience. That childhood memory has now been sharpened and refined by the years. Far from diminishing it has grown in significance and produced genuine thanksgiving. For decades I have known the freedom to do what I most enjoy – preach and share the gospel of the love of God. But along with that freedom has come the awareness that it was purchased at great cost by men and women whose names I read every time I enter our churches. I thank God for those memorial plaques which ensure that we never forget, that we never allow memory to be depreciated or hope to be ridiculed. They are tangible reminders of the true servant of God who, in the words of the psalmist, 'Keeps his oath, even when it hurts'. Ps. 15.5.

The Right Reverend Frank P Sargeant
The Bishop of Stockport
Extracts from a Sermon for Remembrance Sunday

Remembrance today is dominated by the symbol of a red poppy. For some it holds memories of agony or panic as they remember the action. Perhaps they are memories they would prefer to forget. For some like John, who served in the Special Air Service they are memories of young faces. Only nine out of seventy returned from action in the Second World War and only two are alive now. "The bond between us was so strong I would have done anything for any of them" he says. For him the red poppy spells sacrifice; the sacrifice of young lives spent in the cause of justice and peace.

For Helen the poppy stands for the joy of real life and she compares the red of the poppy with the greyness of life in the Second World War with its fears and shortages, and the sheer dread of receiving a letter telling you that your Dad has been killed or taken prisoner.

For Ray, now a clergyman living in retirement, the poppy means liberty. That's what he remembers after four years spent in a Japanese prison camp in the Far East. He prefers to remember the act of freedom rather than the unspeakable miseries he endured. With his liberty he has worked for the welfare of those who suffered, and continue to bear the physical and mental scars.

And, of course, the poppy represents the support for wounded and disabled ex-servicemen and women who need care. We may wear our poppies with pride, but do we wear them with generous compassion?

So far it has been assumed that we shall remember them. We remember them as people and we honour the dead, but we do not honour war. We honour those who remain. It is easy to dismiss those who have lived to tell the tale, sometimes to the point of boredom. "Did I tell you about the time when I was Monty's cook in the desert?" But we honour them because their memories are so powerful and significant, but we do not want either them or ourselves to be trapped in the past.

Of course, there are those who have no memory of the two World Wars and those who fought in them. For them it is just a bit of history. Henri Nouwen, in his book 'Creative Ministry', says something helpful about remembering. He says that those who are not aware of the past cannot celebrate the present. We are brought to where we are today, all of us young and old, by innumerable people who live their lives before we were given our chance to live ours. Many of them lie in war graves in standard rows like troops on parade; some have no X to mark the spot, but are names on memorials and cenotaphs. Nevertheless, in these ways we remember those innumerable people who fought and died in the two World Wars in order that we can live in freedom, and value it.

And so we come to the text. "Remember that you have been called to live in freedom", St Paul says to the Galatians, "but not a freedom that gives free rein to the flesh." We are not to live self-reliantly and selfishly. If we do the outcome is spelt out in verses 19 to 21 of Gal: 5. To live this way is to misuse freedom and hinder justice and love. In contrast if we live in the Spirit, then we shall experience fruits of the Spirit as spelt out in verses 22 and 23. Now we can apply these criteria of the good and bad to discover whether we, as a society and as individuals, are using properly the freedom won for us by those who suffered and died in two World Wars. We shall be saddened, but not surprised by what we find. Certainly those who remain, having fought or having lost loved ones, may well ask "Was it worth it?" And that is a question which Jesus could have asked as he died for us in winning our liberty from sin and death. That is the freedom of which St Paul speaks. Jesus' offering of himself for us was pure gift, and that is how the offering of the lives we remember to-day has to be seen too. It is a gift to live our lives in freedom, but not to misuse it. It is difficult to speak in the same breath of the death of Jesus on the Cross and the fallen of the two World Wars. It is difficult to look at the Cross surrounded by battle scenes of the First World War, like we find in some stained-glass windows, but we recognise this fact. The sacrifice of fellow human beings for love of others brings sharply into focus the love of Jesus in dying for us, and recalls us to the visual centre of our Christian faith. And both events share one significant factor – the value of the sacrifice is to be found in those who remain to live; in you and me, and how we live our lives for others.

Poppies, then, are for remembrance. They are a reminder that as wars continue we have not learnt lessons. They are symbols of how we remember others and what they have done for us. They are a reminder of the cost of freedom to be used in serving others. The most powerful and beautiful poppy is to be found in the Holy Land – at its heart is a cross, the symbol of loving service.

The Right Reverend Brian Smith
The Bishop of Tonbridge

Having been born in 1943, I have no clear childhood memories of the Second World War as it was taking place. Such memories as I have are of the immediate post-war years, including attendance at ceremonies at war memorials either at school or in church. Increasingly I have begun to sense the importance of such acts of remembrance as they take place at a local memorial and are shared in by local people.

Human beings often have difficulty in appreciating the real horror of the effects of war. Despite familiarity with figures and statistics we can still find it difficult to appreciate the extent of the loss of life caused by the two major world wars of this century. Our minds have difficulty in grasping what is implied by statistics that talk simply of 'millions of dead'. An appreciation of the full horror of these wars can come home to us when we stand beside a small village memorial, and realise that from this particular village fifty young men went to war and did not return. And something similar happened in all the villages throughout the country. The war memorials throughout our land highlight the impact that the wars of this century had on our country. They do so by reminding us of the ways those wars affected these very specific communities, made up of these very specific families, who lost these named ones in the conflicts.

Such acts of remembrance, acts in which we remember the dead from our local communities, gives us a picture of the devastating effects of war on to which we can hold. It brings the horror home to us in ways that the reading of statistics never can. Having grasped what war can do, in this very particular and concrete way we realise the constant need to be vigilant in our work for peace.

Britain's darkest hour of modern times was during the summer of 1940. A few brave men protected our freedom and our civilization from Nazi domination; to them we owe eternal thanks. Perhaps the most famous of 'The Few' was Squadron Leader Douglas Bader. When the world forgets such men as this it will inevitably forget the lessons that were learned and open the way to future evil.
(Photo courtesy Imperial War Museum)

CHAPTER SEVEN

INHERITANCE OF THE POST-WAR GENERATIONS

In the first chapter of this book, the Liberty of Liberation was discussed, and its prevelent theme throughout has been of the freedom won for us by the Hero Generation of 1939–45. In a moving speech on 6 June 1994, during the celebrations to mark the 50th Anniversary of D-Day, these few simple words spoken by President Clinton, said it all: "Let us not forget that when they were young, these men saved the World."

In this chapter those who were born at the very end of the war and therefore too young to remember anything of it, and those who have been born since, reflect on their inherited freedom, and the debt which is owed to those who secured it. Also listed here are people who represent the Armed Forces of today and relevent Government departments. The feelings expressed here are perhaps the most important of all, if the act of remembrance is to be maintained into the future. At the end of the day, whether or not Remembrance Sunday is continued into the next century and beyond at its present status, there will be those in towns and villages throughout the land, who will never forget and who will remember in their own capacity. Paramount amongst these will remain the Royal British Legion.

Polly Toynbee

Born in 1946, part of the post-war bulge generation, I always listened deeply moved to my parents' generation's account of their experience of war. We have lived through a unique time of peace but it leaves us in danger of forgetting what war means.

As well as suffering, wars have also been the cornerstones of our history, a way of measuring time. The question for us now is how we in Western Europe should live without it, and keep enough sense of purpose, community, nationhood and common sacrifice for the common good without having to kill each other.

FROM: GENERAL SIR PETER INGE GCB ADC Gen

MINISTRY OF DEFENCE
MAIN BUILDING WHITEHALL LONDON SW1A 2HB

CHIEF OF THE GENERAL STAFF

It is our privilege as serving soldiers, and as the inheritors of this country's proud military tradition, to remember those who served our country in its time of need. There is no greater call demanded of a nation's people than the one which asks them to defend their country and to be prepared to lay down their lives for their fellow countrymen. The courage and dedication of those who have served before us is an inspiration to us and future generations. This tradition of selfless service has endured and many members of her British Army have given their lives in the conflicts which have occurred since the last World War.

It is fitting that the 50th Anniversary of World War Two is remembered, not only for the lives that were lost during the fighting, but for the peace it brought to Europe at its conclusion. It was, however, peace at a price and it is for those who survived, and for the generations which have followed, to count the cost and to continue to keep the peace which our forefathers won for us.

In the quieter moments when I reflect on these matters I can do no better than to echo Laurence Binyon's poignant words which are repeated at memorials in towns and villages across our country every year:

"WE WILL REMEMBER THEM"

Peter Inge

General Sir Peter Inge GCB
Chief of The Defence Staff

It is our privilege as serving soldiers, and as the inheritors of this country's proud military tradition, to remember those who served our country in its time of need. There is no greater call demanded of a nation's people than the one which asks them to defend their country and to be prepared to lay down their lives for their fellow countrymen. The courage and dedication of those who have served before us is an inspiration to us and future generations. This tradition of selfless service has endured and many members of her British Army have given their lives in the conflicts which have occurred since the last World War.

It is fitting that the 50th Anniversary of the Second World War is remembered, not only for the lives that were lost during the fighting, but for the peace it brought to Europe at its conclusion. It was, however, peace at a price and it is for those who survived, and for the generations which have followed, to count the cost and to continue to keep the peace which our forefathers won for us.

In the quieter moments when I reflect on these matters I can do no better than to echo Laurence Binyon's poignant words which are repeated at memorials in towns and villages across our country every year: 'We will remember them'.

Eric Forth MP

Every November people join together in a public act of remembrance and homage to those who died, and were maimed defending our country and its friends. For those not old enough to remember the wars, it is vitally important to ensure continuity of awareness and respect – we must not forget. The values represented by our act of remembrance are eternal, with each generation rededicating themselves every November. It is fitting to see so many of our young people supporting Remembrance Day in every city, town and village. This is the real measure of our respect. After all, so many of those who died were themselves, young.

General Sir Peter de la Billiere

Along with many others of my generation I have fought in wars and conflicts across the world: my father died at the Battle of Crete in 1941 and I have lost many good friends from an early and violent death in the Service of our country.

For those that have not experienced the horrors of war, it is difficult to believe the suffering, disruption and ruination of families and lives that they bring in their wake. If past conflicts and personal sacrifices are to have any lasting contribution for the peace of our world, then the lessons that may be learned both from their causes and their outcome must be carried forward. Future generations will then be grateful for their present freedom and conscious of not repeating mistakes of the past.

My message to the young of today is to say, 'please don't take for granted the peace and security that has been paid for in lives of our servicemen and women; the peace attained by their death is now your responsibility!'

A rare photograph of HMS Fiji, taken in 1940. (Photo courtesy Sir Peter de la Billiere)

Surgeon Lieutenant Commander Claude Dennis Delacour de la Billiere, who was killed in action in 1941 during the Battle of Crete, when HMS Fiji was sunk. 50 years later his son, Lieutenant General Sir Peter de la Billiere was appointed to lead Britain's desert troops during the Gulf War.
(Photo courtesy Sir Peter de la Billiere)

Robert Key MP

I was born in 1945 – a Victory Baby. My father had been rector of Devonport throughout the Second World War and my parents had their house bombed above their heads at the height of the Plymouth blitz. We moved to Salisbury when I was just one year old, so I grew up in a city dominated by uniformed soldiers and vast movements of military vehicles with overhead the drone of propeller-driven aircraft.

There can hardly be a soldier who has not served on Salisbury Plain. Training with the Royal Artillery, in tanks, with the Infantry Regiments, airborne exercises, or nuclear, chemical or biological training – all this and much more is still very much part of our community life in South Wiltshire.

The Royal British Legion has an important and continuing role in our community. Just once a year, on Remembrance Sunday, we all pause to look back. The rest of the year, the RBL is busy looking after the interests of comrades past and present, their families and dependents. Victory in 1945 gave this nation worldwide respect and responsibilities which mean that British military personnel are on active service somewhere in the world for the forseeable future. The British Legion still has a great task to perform, fifty years on.

So in Salisbury we live with our memories – but all around us - and above us – is military activity of which the community is immensely proud. The military depend now on a large and highly-trained civilian workforce.

The sacrifice and the purpose of that great victory fifty years ago lives on all around us in Salisbury. Young and old alike are proud of, and inspired by, the unsung heroes as well as the giants of old.

Douglas French MP

I represent the City of Gloucester. As well as being at the heart of a defence manufacturing region, the City was the home of the Gloucestershire Regiment. The Glorious Glosters are most renowned for their epic stand at Imjin, during the Korean War, where they delayed the Chinese Communist advance towards Seoul and gave the UN forces the vital time they needed to regroup. The 1st Battalion of the Gloucestershire Regiment held their position for three days and nights despite being greatly outnumbered and in isolation. The battalion was virtually wiped out, and the few survivors had to fight their way back to UN lines. Their commanding officer, Colonel James Carne, was awarded the Victoria Cross. Sadly this year the Glosters have been amalgamated as part of the restructuring that is currently underway in our armed forces. I have no doubt however that their heroic spirit will live on as an inspiration to us all.

Baroness Chalker of Wallasey

I was a child of two when the doodlebug fell on our church. It is the only noise of the war I remember. But as a Brownie I helped to raise money for our new church and then as a teenager I was encouraged to build bridges with young Germans. By chance, I was in Berlin when the wall was put up. Now thirty three years later a new life is beginning in that old eastern block.

None of the freedoms slowly helping those eastern countries today would be possible without the freedom for which so many allied troops fought. The task for us all in the 90's and beyond is to understand what Britain fought so well to protect and to teach other nations that the peace we take for granted, can only be protected by democratic vigilance.

My task, and that for all who escaped the horrors, is to work to see they never recur.

Clare Short MP

I was born in 1946 and am probably part of the luckiest generation that ever grew up in Britain. We had peace, liberty, free orange juice, full employment and an enormous sense of hope and optimism about the future. When I was 16, I read Shirer's *Rise and Fall of the Third Reich*. I took on board the enormity of the evil of Hitler's reich. I assumed that everyone had learned the lessons of the evil of racism and anti-semitism. I was shocked later to learn that this was not true. I also appreciated what a terrible error appeasement had been. If Hitler had been stopped earlier, then the cost would have been less. The war was undoubtedly a just war. Those who gave their lives did so that evil could be turned back and decent life resumed. We must always treasure the memory of those who fought in the war. We must honour their courage and their sacrifice and we must be determined that the monstrous ideas that inspired Hitler are never allowed to flourish again and to bring the world to war.

William Waldegrave MP

I come from the first generation that was too young to remember the war from first hand experience but I remember vividly the sense of the achievement of the generations above my own. The Royal British Legion does admirable work in maintaining the memory of those who made the ultimate sacrifice and also – just as important – helping in practical ways those who survived the great Wars and other conflicts. The book of remembrance will, I am sure, be a moving tribute and a worthy one to those who defended freedom with such courage.

Margaret Beckett MP

My memories of the war come only from family stories. What those stories conveyed to me was the way in which people's lives and the nature of their society was utterly changed by the harsh and dramatic experiences of that war, which had such an impact on everyone, from small children to the elderly who remembered the previous Great War.

Rightly, we remember and honour those who made sacrifices, and in some cases, sacrificed their lives in the Armed Services. It was, however, a whole nation, at home and overseas, women as well as men, working in industry, agriculture and in the public services as well as the Armed Forces, on whom the burden of that struggle fell. They deserve to be remembered for their defeat of Fascism. They also deserve our remembrance and our gratitude for the fact that even when exhausted and devastated by war, they then chose not to rest on their laurels, but to work to build a better future for us all.

Lord James Douglas-Hamilton MP

I am delighted that a Golden Book of Remembrance is being prepared. Although I have served nearly ten years as a volunteer I am very much aware that my own generation has been spared the ravages of a great war. It is therefore difficult for some of our children to appreciate the hardship and endeavour which so many of our countrymen had to go through in those traumatic times. It is as well for our children and grandchildren to remember that for our tomorrow many of our countrymen gave their today.

Ann Widdecombe MP

Iwas not born until two years after the war, so the only effects I suffered were those of rationing in my early years! I can remember the end of sweet rationing and being taken along on the gardener's bicycle to buy some sweets. However the victory which was so hard won meant that I grew up in a free country and ever since I have been old enough to understand freedom I have valued it. I missed the war but not the cold war and whenever I contemplated Eastern Europe I could only thank God for Britain's freedom. Of course my parents experienced both wars and my mother tells how she can remember sheltering under the kitchen table as a child during Zeppelin raids over Plymouth. My father spent part of the Second World War at sea or in the Middle East. My brother – aged two – and mother came back from Gibraltar, where my father had been posted, across France just before it fell. The War also accounts for the large gap (ten years) between my brother and myself. My parents would not have another child with the future so uncertain. Hearing all these stories I grew up and seeing around me those who had been injured or disfigured by war, I could identify with that long struggle in which I was not directly involved. I hope future generations will feel a similar identity and that they will never forget what we owe to those who died.

The Viscount Cranborne
Parliamentary Under-Secretary of State for Defence

Even those of us who were born after 1945 have been touched by the two world wars. Every one of us has had a member of our family killed or wounded. We all know people who fought or served. We have grown up on a diet of films and books which themselves reflect the extraordinary impact both wars have had on our way of life, on the way we think, on every aspect of our national existence. The impact has been greater than that of the Thirty Years' War on Germany, or the wars of Napoleon on western Europe.

Nevertheless, the world moves on. Many younger people in our country now do not know about those two cataclysmic events. Many do not want to know. Technology is increasingly relegating the past to an attic we do not visit except as a setting for a television drama, in spite of the best efforts of modern museum directors.

In those two world wars our country exhausted itself in an expenditure of men and treasure that had hitherto been unimaginable. It did so in a good cause: survival against barbarism. We owe it to those who fought and died to remember them in gratitude for what they did. We also owe it to ourselves. For in remembering them we may save ourselves from a new barbarism that this time threatens us, not from abroad, but from inside each one of us.

The Viscount Astor
Minister of War Pensions, Department of Social Security

It is a particular honour for me to be the Minister for War Pensions as we come to commemorate the 50th anniversary of the end of the Second World War.

Although I was born after those monumentous events, my role as a Minister enables me to meet and talk to survivors of that war. The important work that organisations like the Royal British Legion are doing to care for war pensioners, not only from the Second World War, but from subsequent wars, has shown me that this nation will never forget the brave men and women who fought for the ideals of freedom and democracy.

All governments acknowledge the debt owed to the memory of the men and women who sacrificed their lives in the War. It is this Government's duty to honour that memory and to provide help and assistance, where necessary, for their colleagues injured in the line of duty and unable to return to normal life and for the women who were left widowed.

By the time of the 50th anniversary, my department's War Pensions Agency will have been established for a year. The agency exists to deal specifically with our commitments to all war pensioners and their dependents. It administers the payment of war disablement pensions and it also provides welfare services and support to war disablement pensioners, war widows, their dependents and their carers.

We will never forget those who fell in the War. In my capacity as a Minister, I will endeavour to ensure that future generations will continue to acknowledge the debt we as a nation owe to their memory.

Patrick McLoughlin MP

I am too young to have experienced the Second World War or any of its effects on our lives in the ten years or so after it. We have had peace in this country throughout my life and this, in no small measure, has been due to the victory that was won in 1945. We can never repay those who laid down their lives in that War and the First World War and those of us who are young and never suffered wartime should always remember the debt we owe to ex-servicemen.

Jeremy Hanley MP

Minister of State for The Armed Forces

As Minister of State for the Armed Forces, I have the privilege of working closely with men and women who are dedicated to defending our freedom, territorial integrity and national interests at home and abroad. They meet challenges and hazards in a way which inspires public admiration and professional respect throughout the world. In doing so they are carrying on a fine tradition of service, a tradition exemplified by those who defended freedom and justice in the Second World War.

Anyone who turns the pages of a book of remembrance such as this cannot fail to be moved by the strength of feelings conveyed in the words of gratitude and tribute offered by a wide range of people. There could not, at the time of the Second World War, have been a single family in the nation which escaped the fear, deprivation and uncertainty of those years. Yet this was also a time when so many of our people – Service and civilian – produced their finest achievements. Sometimes, inevitably, they also made the ultimate sacrifice. It is fitting that at this time of anniversary we should remember the efforts of all those involved in that epic conflict – and proudly nurture and encourage that spirit of remembrance.

In recalling those who fell we must not forget those who now grow old and we are thankful for the tireless work of the Royal British Legion and the other ex-Service organisations which have the interests of Service veterans at heart.

Our humble and heart-felt act of remembrance serves as a tribute to all those brave men and women who sacrificed everything so that our way of life could be preserved, free from tyranny. They have the honour which is their due. We must never forget them.

General Sir Charles Huxtable KCB CBE
President of the Ex-Services Mental Welfare Society

It is now 50 years since the ending of the Second World War and 76 since the end of the First World War, and yet we still remember. Many people ask 'Is this right? Should we not now forgive and forget?' In my opinion it is not a question of forgiving, that happened a long time ago, but how can we forget, when we remain surrounded by those who are still suffering as casualties, particularly from the Second World War and indeed from all the other actions in which British forces have been involved since 1945.

We in the Ex-Services Mental Welfare Society, founded 75 years ago to help in the restoration to health of those suffering mental illness as a result of their service in those terrible conditions experienced by so many in World War I, find that, although the last of the veterans from that war in our care passed away in 1990 at the age of 98, there is a continuing need for our help. In the first 75 years of our history we have assisted 60,000 ex-members of the Services, even today the Society is providing help for some 3,800 veterans. We provide this help through a veterans' home, two short stay treatment centres and a network of Welfare Officers throughout the country who visit, help, advise and cheer our clients.

It is because of this continuing need to care for such injured veterans that we must continue to remember. It is not just a matter of waiting for old veterans to die so that the job is finished, we already have some 40 members on our books from the South Atlantic (Falklands) campaign and a steady trickle from Northern Ireland. These are young people, part of our Nation today, they are not old dinosaurs to be left to fade away quietly, they are a living body of people who have given their health for our security and we all need to remember and sustain them.

The Baroness Blatch CBE

It is so very important that the freedom that was fought for and won by men and women, many of them very young, both at home and abroad, is recognised and remembered by all of us.

I believe it is especially important that the young people of today understand the nature of the struggle against Fascism and the significance of its defeat.

The sacrifices were great and the victory poignant.

As someone who served in the Womens Royal Air Force, who married a Royal Air Force test pilot, and now the proud mother of a daughter and son-in-law who both serve in the RAF, I have an appreciation of the need to protect our freedom.

I remain hopeful. The impact on us all, but particularly young people of the D-Day commemoration activities this year was profound.

We must Never Forget.

Patrick Nicholls MP

One of my most vivid memories of the House of Commons occurred in 1987. I was having dinner with two MPs, both of these were standing down in the forthcoming election. One had just returned from a visit to Berlin and remarked that generals were now looking as young as policemen. Our companion agreed. They were both of a generation that had fought in the war, or so I thought.

What emerged was that the one, recently returned from Germany, had fought throughout the war, retiring with the acting rank of Lieutenant Colonel. The other, by contrast, celebrated VE Day at school. There were just six years between them in age. It is at times almost impossible for anyone who has not lived through those times to comprehend what it must have been like. My parents-in-law were talking to my elder daughter recently and they were trying to convey what it was like to meet each other briefly on leave in London, in the acute realisation that within weeks London might be under German occupation.

How many of those who complain fashionably about the bombing of Hiroshima and Nagasaki dare to confront the fact that VJ day would have been delayed for at least a year? My father in law, after fighting in Europe was about to be shipped out East and to what fate? I have no complaints to make that the war was brought to an end by the nuclear bomb.

For those who lived and fought, for those who merely waited, there must at times be a feeling that those of us who remain have no idea of the debt we owe. Speaking for myself, I do not believe that is true. When at each Remembrance Day Service in Shaldon, I hear the names of the fallen read out, the fact that they died before I was even born does not lessen the pathos of the occasion and we make a serious mistake in believing that the young cannot be brought to an understanding of why they are free today.

Andrew Faulds MP

A Book of Remembrance gives us the opportunity, indeed requires the duty, to recall the appalling sacrifices that so many thousands of our young men and their maturer colleagues made fifty years ago in the war to destroy the power and evil of German Nazism and Italian Fascism. Sadly we too readily forget the sufferings of the dead and wounded and the tragedy for their families.

After the war, we all believed in Britain that we could create, as a political outcome, a society which would show more care and concern for all in our community, that would entail a fairer economic spread and that would extend political power more widely. To the degree that we have failed in that endeavour, we have diminished the contribution that our war dead made to ensure the spread of democracy and to change the political pattern of the world across large areas of the globe. Our greatest failure would be to allow any form of fascism to rise again and invalidate their struggle and their sacrifice.

David Maclean MP

I belong to the generations who could so easily forget; no memories of the war or of families torn apart by it; brought up in an era of increasing prosperity where real deprivation is not understood; where real heroes have become replaced with superficial media personalities and the greatest sacrifice most of us are asked to make is to empty the dishwasher. In this oh so cynical, sophisticated world, where all our cherished institutions are mocked, denigrated or taken for granted, one thing stands out like an untarnished beacon – the outstanding professionalism of our armed forces, embodying all that is best in mankind and in our country. Their devotion to duty and integrity have not changed. They have not grown old. In today's armed forces we can see the same people who went to war in 1939. They are the living tribute to those who made the supreme sacrifice and every time we take credit in their past achievements we are honouring the memories of those who went before and those who died in battles, whether or not they are on the Regimental Colours.

As a young officer in the 51st Highland Volunteers, I will never forget attending a presentation of the Battle of Wadi Akarit in North Africa. There was a civilian present – a soft-spoken Highland gentleman who reminded me of an old uncle. The Adjutant concluded the presentation by reading the extraordinary citation for the VC awarded to the CO of the 7th Argyll and Sutherland Highlanders. This officer, though wounded and in great pain, stood in the open under a hail of enemy fire, directing the fighting with utter disregard for his personal safety. His refusal to be evacuated for medical help inspired his whole Battalion and, as the citation says, 'This officer's gallantry and magnificent leadership when his now tired men were charging the enemy with the bayonet and were fighting them to hand grenade range, are worthy of the highest honour and can seldom have been surpassed in the long history of the Highland Brigade'. The Adjutant then called on the old highlander to rise and introduce him as Lt. Col. Lorne Campbell VC, the CO of the 7th Argylls. No-one present will forget that moment and I am confident that the vast majority of our people will continue to appreciate the need for remembrance. When we start to forget the last war we bring forward the date of the next.

But we will not forget for another reason also; because in all of those who made the supreme sacrifice we see a little bit of ourselves as we would like us to be. They died for honour, duty, country and freedom. If we deny their remembrance we are denying that we can aspire to their ideals. Yet we know our young people today in our armed forces can proudly carry that same burden and the rest of us glory in their achievements. Every act of pride in our present armed forces is an act of remembrance for those who have gone before. Every time we think of ourselves we will remember them.

Tim Eggar MP

I was born in 1951, so my first real awareness of the threat to peace was the Cuban Missile Crisis.

Yet the Legion forms part of my earliest memories. My

father, at the annual Remembrance Sunday Parade at my home village in Derbyshire; my own role as a cub and then a scout in the annual parades when I was at school in Worcestershire.

Within the last ten years, I have attended the Remembrance Day Service in the Falklands and visited, with my family, the Normandy beaches and the First World War battlefields. I have seen the excellent work done by the Royal British Legion in Enfield. It is not just on Remembrance Day Sunday, but every day that we should recognise that freedom cannot be taken for granted.

Lord Strathclyde

I was not born until long after the war so do not share the memories of other contributors.

My generation has heard the stories from our parents and grandparents, we have read the books and seen the films.

But for today's generation war is something that happens in other lands rather than our own. When we see the guns, the bombed buildings, the people scurrying for their lives within the sights of snipers and when we see the pain and suffering of the wounded and the dying we are filled with horror. Of all the many wars that are happening in the world today, the one with which we are most familiar is that which is happening in Europe.

The stability and the decades of peace which we, in this part of Europe enjoy, was won for us by those who fought for us and by those who gave their lives so that we could be free and at peace today. We must never forget their sacrifice, we must always remember and be grateful.

Nick Harvey MP

Having been born long after the end of the Second World War, I am of the generation which knew nothing of its suffering, nor of the difficult times in our country which both preceded and followed it.

The 'baby boomers' of the 1960s were born in relatively

prosperous and undoubtedly peaceful times and it is we and those who have come since who must beware of disregarding the significance of the sacrifice made by those who went before us.

We take so many liberties and comforts entirely for granted. But our television screens and newspapers which tell so often of the horrors and agonies endured by people in other parts of the world, should serve continually to remind us that there have been times when such dangers and agonies were a reality very much nearer to home.

Young men and women gave up all that they valued and treasured, and many never got to see the modern developments which have so enhanced our quality of life. On the occasion of the Fiftieth Anniversary of the end of the war it must be right for all of us to pause for thought, and remember the incalculable debt we owe to them.

Michael Portillo MP

I am part of the post-war generation, those people whose knowledge of world war comes mainly from hearing of their parents' experiences in battle or in the blitz.

My generation remembers not the war itself but the deep reverence shown during the Remembrance Days of my childhood when all traffic stopped and people in the streets bowed their heads in the silence between the guns.

That generation feels as much as our parents' the value of the freedom and democracy that were fought for and saved. We did not see the horror, but we do know of the sacrifice and we give thanks for the precious gift of liberty made to us by those who gave their lives.

Alistair Burt MP

I am fortunate enough to have been born and brought up in the constituency I represent, the towns of Bury, Tottington and Ramsbottom. There is a lengthy military history to our area, which over the years has provided many men and women to all branches of the armed forces. Most notably the town is remembered for its contribution to the Lancashire Fusiliers. Bury Parish Church is the garrison church still of the Lancashire Fusiliers, and many of its colours are laid up there. The feeling for the Services runs deep in the town and I believe we are the only place in the country which has an annual service and parade to mark Gallipoli Day, remembered in Bury for the contribution of the Lancashire Fusiliers who famously won six VCs before breakfast.

I am also fortunate not to have had the need to serve in uniform to defend my country. Born in 1955 and enjoying the privileges of peace, I know from the history of my home town how dearly that peace was bought for me. The Second World War will be remembered for ever as a clear example of the forces of good having to be mobilised to defeat the forces of evil. The cost was great, both at home and abroad. I am privileged to serve some of those who took part in such stirring events, as well as looking after those born subsequently. We have a great debt to honour, and I hope that the 50th anniversary of the end of the Second World War will be duly recognised by all those fortunate enough to have been spared its ultimate price.

Sebastian Coe OBE MP

I am very much a product of the post war generation and have only the memories of ex-servicemen and women, who are now some times well over 70 years of age, to remind me about the horrors of both world wars and subsequent conflicts around the world where British troops have served.

For many years now I have taken part in the Act of Remembrance on Remembrance Sunday. I have been very much moved by the large number of young people who have also taken part in solemn acknowledgment to the sacrifice of their grandparents and parents.

I pay tribute to the Royal British Legion and other ex-service charitable organisations for all the splendid work they do in helping to alleviate distress among all veterans of the 20th century.

CHAPTER EIGHT

ROYAL BRITISH LEGION
AND THE FUTURE

*Compiled from the Royal British Legion
Festival of Remembrance brochure*

The Royal British Legion was formed in 1921 by bringing together the national organisations of ex-Servicemen which were set up as a result of the First World War, in order to make the most effective use of their resources, recognising that the public would prefer to give their allegiance to a major umbrella organisation caring for the ex-Service community.

The Legion is an active participant in the Council of British Service and Ex-Service Organisations (COBSEO), which represents more than 60 organisations. It is a founder member of the British Commonwealth Ex-Services League (BCEL) and a member of the World Veterans' Federation (WVF), where it discharges its responsibilities both within and beyond the Commonwealth.

The objectives of the Legion include: (1) Promoting the welfare of both serving and ex-Service men and women, and their dependants, and relieving hardship where it exists. (2) Raising and distributing money for these purposes.

The Legion's Charter requires that its responsibility extends to all members of the Service and ex-Service community, regardless of membership of the Legion.

Every Legion branch has associated with it a voluntary local Welfare Committee, composed of Legion representatives and others from the ex-Service and welfare associations in the locality, including the DHSS.

The task of these Committees is to be a confidential contact with ex-Service people, widows and dependants needing help.

Each Committee has direct access to the central benevolent fund (the Poppy Appeal) with authority to give immediate on-the-spot help with basic needs to individual cases. Extra needs are referred to Legion Headquarters who often deal with them in conjunction with other Funds and Associations. They also give

184

preliminary advice on War Pension claims.

The Legion's Headquarters are responsible for controlling and allocating an annual income in excess of £1 million through Departments providing benevolent and welfare services to the whole ex-Service community. Advice is readily available from these Departments.

The Legion offers a comprehensive range of services to all ex-Service men and women and their dependants.

The Legion's Pensions Department deals with more than 16,000 War Pension cases each year, including representations made by a team of trained and experienced officers, free of charge, at 2,600 War Pension Appeal Tribunals. A major task is to identify and provide justification for those entitled to claim a War Pension for a condition attributed to service in the Forces or, for a widow, a condition which may have resulted in or hastened her husband's death. The Department's officers are the acknowledged experts on War Pensions, having a section which provides advice for other ex-Service and welfare organisations.

The Department is also responsible for a Business Advisory Service to assist unemployed ex-Service personnel by giving guidance on setting up businesses and providing interest-free loans. It also runs one of the Legion's employment schemes, The Royal British Legion Taxi Drivers' Training School, which teaches ex-Service personnel to become London taxi drivers. One in three of London's cabbies have passed through it.

The War Graves Pilgrimages Department arranges tours, with medical cover and accommodation, for widows and relatives wishing to visit Military cemeteries in Europe and other parts of the world. They administer the Government's War Widows Grant Scheme, enabling War Widows who have not done so, at Government expense, to visit their husband's grave or memorial overseas.

The Legion is the largest private employer of disabled people. It has six Associated Companies which, whilst operating under the aegis of the RBL, are separate incorporated charities. Amongst the Companies are:

• The RBL Attendants Company Limited. This is a car-parking and security organisation which provides employment for around 1,000 ex-Service people as security guards and car park attendants throughout the country.

• The RBL Industries (Preston Hall) Incorporated. Situated in the Royal British Legion Village, Maidstone, Kent, the Industries not only employ ex-Service personnel who are unable to work in normal industrial conditions, but also place them elsewhere in sheltered industrial groups. In the Industries, they make timber pallets, produce road signs and run modern printing presses. Excellent accommodation is available to them, as well as to applicants during assessment of their potential.

• The RBL Disabled Men's Industries Limited. This Company is also located at the Royal British Legion Village, and was formed to market products made in their own homes by severely-disabled ex-Service men and women.

Two other organisations which have ties with the Legion are:

• The Cambrian Factory. Located at Llanwrtyd Wells, the Factory provides sheltered employment for disabled ex-Service men and women in the manufacture of a wide variety of textiles, including skirts, jackets, scarves and caps.

• The Officers' Association – The Officers' Benevolent Department of The Royal British Legion. Situated at the Headquarters of the Legion in 48 Pall Mall, London SW1Y 5JY, The Officers' Association is concerned with the welfare of ex-Service officers and their dependants, and runs a Resettlement and Employment Department, a Relief Department and a Residential Home.

• The Benevolent Department administers some 3,500 local Welfare Committees throughout the UK, excluding Scotland which has an organisation similar to the Legion. More than 20,000 voluntary workers are helping families in time of crisis; providing extra fuel for the elderly; visiting long-term sick in hospitals and at home; arranging convalescence, and advising on homes for the elderly and incapacitated.

The Department also administers five Legion Residential Homes for life-long care, with a sixth being planned. Three Convalescent Homes accommodate 4,000 visitors each year.

A separate office disburses grants to Polish ex-Servicemen on behalf of the Ministry of Defence.

• The Churchill Centre, built at the Royal British Legion Village, in the Legion's Diamond Jubilee Year (1981), is a purpose-built rehabilitation and assessment centre, with excellent facilities, including a hydrotherapy pool and a gymnasium.

Another two of the six Associated Companies are:

• The RBL Housing Association Limited. This Company provides modern housing accommodation for ex-Servicemen and their wives, as well as for the widows of ex-Servicemen.

Since its inception it has provided homes for 18,000 people. The Head Office is at Penn, High Wycombe, Bucks.

• The Legion Leasehold Housing Association. Located at Gerrards Cross, Bucks, the Association provides good quality low-cost, warden-assisted retirement housing for leasehold purchase.

The Women's Section not only runs its own Homes and Schemes, but also plays a vital role in the Poppy Appeal and in many Legion Branch Welfare Committees which attend to the needs of the local ex-Service community and visit the sick and the elderly in hospitals and at home.

Young people of ex-Service families are sponsored by the Legion for Outward Bound courses and Sail Training Association cruises. The RBL also supports the United World Colleges, through the Earl Mountbattten Scholarship, and a variety of other youth activities, including bands. The RBL is affiliated to the British Youth Band Association.

The Legion's Benevolent Fund is dependent on the worldwide Poppy Appeal collections which are organised by the Appeals Department with the help of some 5,000 organisers and 300,000 collectors, all of whom give their services voluntarily. There is always an urgent need for more collectors and for other volunteers to help with fund-raising activities.

If you can help in any way, please contact the Appeals Secretary, The Royal British Legion, Royal British Legion Village, Maidstone, Kent ME20 7NX.

Forty million poppies, as well as 80,000 wreaths and 250,000 Remembrance crosses, are made annually at The RBL Poppy Factory in Richmond, Surrey TW10 6UR, employing disabled ex-Service men and women. This is the sixth of the Legion's Associated Companies.

There are some eight million ex-Service men and women, and their ten million dependants, some now in their 80s, who may need help. All are eligible for the Legion's assistance – no less than one-third of the entire population.

If you would like to visit any of the Legion's Homes or companies, please get in touch with the Department concerned. They will be pleased to meet you. If in doubt, please contact the General Secretary.

The Legion would also welcome enquiries from any ex-

Service, or Campaign, association who are interested in joining forces with the Legion. In this way, their continuation could be assured. Enquiries should be made to the General Secretary, The Royal British Legion, 48 Pall Mall, London SW1Y 5JY.

The Royal British Legion
PRINCIPLES AND POLICY

The Legion shall be democratic, non-sectarian and not affiliated to or connected directly with any political organisation.

The Legion shall be created to inaugurate and maintain in a strong, stimulating, united and democratic comradeship all those who have served in Her Majesty's Navy, Army, Air Force or any Auxiliary Forces so that neither their efforts nor their interests shall be forgotten, that their welfare and that of the dependants of the fallen may be safeguarded and that just and equitable treatment shall be secured to them in respect of the difficulties caused in their lives as a result of their services.

The Legion shall exist to perpetuate in the civil life of the Commonwealth and the World the principles for which the Nation stands, to inculcate a sense of loyalty to the Crown, Community and Nation, to promote unity amongst all classes, to make right the master of might, to secure peace and goodwill on earth, to safeguard and transmit to posterity the principles of justice, freedom and democracy and to consecrate and sanctify our comradeship by our devotion to mutual service and helpfulness.

In this photograph taken during the Commemorative Act of Remembrance at Portland on 25 May 1994, the Bishop of Sherborne (Bishop to Her Majesty's Forces) is nearest the camera. On his left is the Chaplain, the Reverend Richard Buckley and fourth along from him is the Rt. Hon. Winston Churchill MP, another contributor to The Golden Book of Remembrance.

Subscribers

to the

GOLDEN BOOK

OF

REMEMBRANCE

This book has been published thanks to the support
and encouragement given by the subscribers
listed on the following pages.

A

Abbott, Godfrey; Captain, Royal Irish Rangers.
Adlington, Miss J.M.
Anthony, K.W.; 295303 Cpl of Horse, 1st Life Guards and Desert Rats.
Armstrong, Jeff; RAF, GSC, NSM, MA.

B

Baker, Basil; 13/18 Royal Hussars, North Irish Horse.
Ball, Albert E; Sapper, Royal Engineers. Italian Star, Defence Medal, 1939-45 Star, WW2 King's Medal for Wounded and Disabled.
Beards, Mrs L; Sister Melland MPNS.
Bingley, Adrian; SAC, RAF, ROC.
Blair, Bert.
Blunsden, K.H.; WOII, 1st Blazers R.A.
Bennet House, Royal British Legion Rest & Convalescence Home, Co. Antrim, Northern Ireland.
Bond, J.H.; Pte, Suffolk Regiment, Palestine General Service Medal 1938, North-west Frontier Indian Service Medal 1939, Burma Star 1942-44, 1939-45 Star, 1939-45 Medal, Defence Medal, General Service Cross.
Bourne, J.D.; Major, Royal Artillery.
Brandish, J.R.; WO, RAF.
Bradbury, Alan.
Bray, W.H.; Survey Engineer, Royal Engineers.
Brewer, Ronald S.; Special Operator, 'Y2' Normandy, R.C. of Signals Mobile.
Bridge, K.B.; Pte, Queen's Royal Regiment, 1st Batallion. 7th Indian Division, 14th Army. 1939-45 Star, Burma Star, Defence Medal, Victory Medal.
Brightman; Vitéz Sgt John Brightman, Royal Hungarian Armed Forces. The Knightly Order of Vitéz (16.9.84), The Small Silver and Bar, The Bronze and Bar, 1st Class Hungarian Campaign Cross with Swords and Wreath and 2 Wounded Bars, 2nd Class German Iron Cross (E.K. 2 Classe).
Brightman, Olive Mary; LAC/W, WAAF. Defence Medal.
Brunt, Charles Eric; Driver/Mechanic, 326-64th A.T. Regiment Royal Artillery C.M.A. 8th Army.
Bunch, F.S. 5505348; Pte, Queen's Own Royal West Kent Regiment, 16.5.40 to 31.3.46.
Bush, A.E.; 4390209, Gunner, 21st Anti-Tank, Royal Artillery.

C

Carrington, Raymond D.; Captain, JP, Queen's Royal Regiment, Gold Cross of Merit (Rep Pol.).
Chapman, George; Sgt 1939-46, Irish Guards, RAF, RAF Regiment, 1946-62 British Fire Service.
Chubb, Peter; Guardsman, Coldstream Guards.
Clarke, M.S.; Major, Royal Artillery, MBE.
Clarke, R.C.; Sgt, Bedfordshire Yeomanry.
Clee, F.W.; 14340449, Pte, 5th Battalion, East Yorkshire Regiment, 1939-45 Star, France-Germany Star, Defence Medal, War Medal 1935-45.
Clipston, J.R.; WO1 (RSM), 3 RHA.

Collis, Charles T.; AB, Russian Convoys B.O. Atlantic C/JX394843 D.E.M.S. RN.

Cook, J.N.; CSM/WOII, Worcestershire Regiment (Burma).

Cooper, William, 14397; CSM, D.C.M 8th North Staffs Regiment 1914-1919.

Cooper, William Thomas, 143251829; Cpl, Royal Warwickshire Regiment 1939-1945.

Cowan, N, 2118800; LACW, WRAF.

Crompton, Roderick; Specialist, The Loyal Regiment G.S.C.

D

Dalton, A.

Dare, R.H.; Sgt, Royal Corps of Signals.

Davey, A.; Major, 3rd Battalion, Monmouthshire Regiment, 11th Armoured Division, C.D.G.

Davis, Miss B.E.

Deakin, Mrs D.

Densham-Booth, D.F.; Lt-Col, Royal Engineers, OBE.

Desborough, Ms M.E.; 2147832 LAC/W, WRAF

Dodd, Ms E.E.; 2828212 AC/W, WRAF.

Douglas, David; Sgt, Royal Scots Guards, MM.

Driver, Frank Kenneth; 806766, AB, RN.

Dunker, Douglas S.; S/N, RAFVR

Dunnico, E.S.; Cpl, RAF.

Durey, J.E.; CSM, Rifle Brigade, 1939-45 Star, Africa Star, Italy Star, France-Germany Star, Defence Medal, 1939-45 Victory Medal, Oak Leaves, Mentioned in Despatches.

Dyke, Richard; Sapper, Royal Engineers, 1939-45 Star, France-Germany Star, Defence Medal.

E

Emary, M.; Commander, RN.

Eslick, K.G.; LAC, RAF

F

Farmery, Raymond; ISM, East Yorks ROC.

Fitness, Edward William; Sgt, Coldstream Guards 1939-46.

Fitness, Graham.

Fitzgerald, K.J.; WO1(RSM), 1st Devon & Dorset Regiment.

Flanagan, J.C.; 21182024, Sgt, 35 LAA S/L Regiment, Royal Artillery.

Flanagan, M.R.; 23144849, Bombadier, 26th Field Regiment, Royal Artillery.

Floyd, Keith.

Framingham, A.; Leading Seaman, RN.

Frieberg, Mrs U.

Fryer; W/288626 Cpl, ATS. BAOR.

G

Gale, D.P.; LAC, Bomber Command, RAF.

Garrett, D.

Geary, T.H.; WO, RCAF, 405 & 159 Squadrons, DFC.

Gillan, Robert C.; 2nd Battalion, Rifle Brigade. DCM.
Gillman, David L.; Cpl, Music Services, RAF, 1952-64; T.A. Musician 1965-71; Royal Observer Corps 1972-91. Coronation Medal 1953, General Service Medal (Cyprus) 1958-61, Royal Observer Corps Medal 1972-84.
Glanvill, Catherine: Major, RAMC. OBE, O.St.J, MB, BS, MRCGP, MICD;
Glanvill, Dr. Terry; Major, RAMC, Medical Officer of 6th Airborne Para Field Ambulance. TD, C.St.J, BA, MRCGP, FICD.
Graham, Michael; WO1(ASM), REME.
Gray, A.C.; s/211586/w Sgt, RASC.
Gregory, Neil; P/JX577275, Telegraphist, RN Combined Operations.
Gregson, R.W.; Gunner, 6 Medium Regiment, Royal Artillery.
Griffits, Peter; BA, M.Phil.

H

Hale, William Edward; Royal Corps of Signals.
Hanford, M.G.; s/23461553, RASC BAOR 12, BFPO 17.
Harrop, Reverend Prebendary J.B.; Captain, Worcestershire Regiment and SDF.
Harvey, Joseph Cowan; LAC, RAF.
Hill, George; Quartermaster, North Staffs Regiment, BEM, TD.
Hilton, E.; 2113606 Cpl, 575 A/T Company, Royal Engineers - Gibralter, France, India.
Hobbs, Geoffrey Stanton; 146711119 Cpl, Durham Light Infantry.
Hope, T.; Sgt, 8CCS, Royal Army Medical Corps. MBE.
Hughes, James; Colonel, Royal Artillery, CBE, TD, DL.
Hughes, Mrs Maureen.

I

Isted, W.J.; Petty Officer PTI, RN.

J

Jacob, Ernest M.; Cpl, Royal Engineers.
Jull, Sydney James; Flying Officer, 138 and 35 Squadrons, RAF

K

Kearns, J.; Pte, Pioneer Corps.
Kew, A.J.W.; 2658443 Sgt, Coldstream Guards 1937-46. 8th Army in North Africa, Italy and Palestine. Palestine Medal, 1939-45 Star, Africa Star, Italy Star, Defence Medal, 1939-45 Medal.
Kew, Mrs I., A.T.S 1941-46, 1939-45 Star, Defence Medal, 1939-45 Medal.
Killingsley-Smith, Grenadier Guards 1956-59.
Kingston, T.; Driver, Royal Army Service Corp, Royal Engineers.

L

Laird, Mr & Mrs Ian Watson.
Lait, R.; Petty Officer.
Langley, Kenneth; Gunner, 14th Division, Royal Artillery.
Langlois, H.E.; AB, RN 1939-45.
Laundon, J.L.; Pte, ATT, 96th Field Regiment, RDYA.
Lawrence, Alfred Henry George; P/JX178849, RN 1940-46.

Leigh, William K.; RSM/SRS, DSC, DCM, MM.
Le Marquand, Linden; Lt-Commander, RNVR.
Leonard, V.J.; Pte, Parachute Regiment.
Lloyd, K.W.N.; Sgt, 47 Air Despatch Squadron.
Long, W.B.J., Cpl, RAF. Malaysia, Arabian Peninsular, North Africa. GSM.
Love, T.J.; 22960432, Cpl, Royal Engineers.

M

Mann, Richard Antony; Seaman, RN. HMS Nimrod.
Martin, Miss G.; 2143971 SAC/W, WAAF/WRAF 1943-1951.
Mattingley, W.R.; F/Sgt, RAF.
Mayne, A.J.M.; 504/2194 Sgt, 4th Infantry Brigade, 21st Army Group. War
    Volunteer Medal, Commemorative Medal 1939-45.
Mayor, L.A.; Rifleman, Cameronians (Scottish Rifles).
Meeghan, John Christopher; Merchant Navy. 1939-45 Medal, 1939-45 Star,
    Atlantic Star, France-Germany Star, Commemorative Medal (from the
    people of Normandy). Took part in the Normandy invasion aged 15 years
    and 2 months.
Menken, Carl R.; Boy Rating, Merchant Navy. 1939-45 Star, Atlantic Star,
    France-Germany Clasp, War Medal.
Metcalfe, Harry; 23442859 Pte, 1st Battalion, Prince of Wales Own Regiment of
    Yorkshire.
Molyneux, Anthony; Pte, Loyals.
Moore, J.H.; Sgt Pilot, FMA.RAFVR, 1940-46.
Morden, Peggie F; WRVS Services Welfare Administrator, UK, 1940-64. MBE.
Morgan, Doris M.; 443458 Cpl. MBE

N

Nash, Edward C.; Cpl, RASC, Waterborne (Norway).
Nash, M.T.; Sgt, ACC Para.
Nash, Peter; RAF, RAFVR, Royal Observer Corps, Air Training Cops.
Noble, J.F.; Major, Parachute Regiment.
Norton, Frank William; Flt. Lt., 203 Squadron, RAF.

P

Pennington, H.W.; Signalman, Royal Signals.
Peters, Jurek, Polish Army.
Plant, F.S.; Sgt, Berkshire Yeomanry, Royal Artillery.
Polland, George; Cpl, RAMC 1923-45.
Pollicott-Reid, P.J.; RAAF, Royal Observer Corps.
Potter, R.
Prunty, J.

Q

Quaedvlier, J.A.M.A.; Navigation Officer, Merchant Navy following Netherlands
    underground. 1939-45 Star, France-Germany Star, War Medal 1939-45.
    Dutch decorations: War Memorial Cross, Resistance Memorial Cross,
    Netherlands Underground Forces Medal, Olympic Cross.

R

Read, Douglas R.; WO, RAF. BEM.

Reed, Eric C.; Driver, RASC.

Reed, Maggy.

Renard, Louis C.; élite soldier, 21st Army Group, 4th Brigade in Northern Ireland. Military Combat Medal 1940-45, Volunteer War Medal 1940-45, Rhine Army Cross, Commemorative Medal 1940-45, GSC, Cross of Knight of the Order of Leopold.

Riche, T.J.F.; Pte, NSM, GSC, VSM.

Ridley, G.; 81820333638 Pte, RAMC.

Ridley, W.A.; 644290 Sgt, RAF.

Roberts, T.P.; Cpl, RAMC. Korea (U.N.), Malaysia.

Rogers, Raymond V.; 5339481, 4th Battalion, Royal Berkshire Regiment. 1939-45 Star, Defence Medal, War Medal, Territorial Long Service Medal, National Service Medal 1939-46, Dunkirk Medal.

S

Saxelby, R.; Pte, 2 platoon, 1 section, 6th Airborne.

Scammell, S.J.; Gunner.

Scott, J.C.A.; 14424447 Sgt, RAOC, BAOR.

Scott, W.J.; Pte, Gloucestershire Regiment.

Shrubbs, Mrs Joyce; Royal Observer Corps. MBE.

Skinner, William M.; Sapper, REME 1941-46.

Smith, Edward W.; 2320629 Cpl.

Smith, R.E.; NAI LFX635180, 1943-52.

Smith, Mrs R.E. (née Gregory); 440740 LAC/W, 1940-43.

Smith, Reginald Gordon; Petty Officer, RN.

Soden, E.J.; 6200167 WOII (CSM), Middlesex Regiment; TA London Infantry Brigade. 1939-45 Star, Pacific Star, Defence Medal, War Medal, Coronation Medal, Good Conduct Medal (18 years Service).

Southwell, J.H.; Cpl RDT, RADC.

Standing, A.D.M.; Major.

Staples, A.E.; Pte, 1st Battalion, Queen's Own Royal West Kent Rifles.

Steere, R.; T/230894 Cpl.

Stevens, J.G.; Driver, RASC.

Stevens, Richard W.; Cpl of Horse, Household Cavalry Regiment, The Life Guards. 1939-45 Star, Africa Star, Defence Medal, War Model 1939-45, Arabian Peninsular Medal, Long Service & Good Conduct Medal, George Cross Medal.

Stone, R.B.; Cpl, 14 Coy, RASC. 1939-45 Star, Africa Star, 8th Army Clasp, Italy Star, Defence Medal, Victory Medal.

T

Taylor, H.R.; Major, Royal Artillery.

Taylor, J.; Sapper, Royal Engineers.

Thirlwell, P.W.; LEM (Air), RN. General Service Medal, Near East Medal (Suez).

Tiley, A.E.; 1097318 Gunner, 513 Battery, 149 A/T Regiment, Royal Artillery, 4th India Division.

Tovey, V.W.; Pte, Royal Warwickshire Regiment and REME. Belgian Croix de Guerre.
Turner, J.E.; Observer Officer (W), 16 Group, ROC.

V

Van Overstraeten, Charles E.
Varney, E.K.; C/Obs.

W

Wall, John; S/Sgt, 27th Armoured Brigade.
Wall, Thomas A.E.; Sgt, Irish Guards.
Walker, Frank; 23347665 Gunner, 58th Med Regiment, Royal Artillery.
Warwick, Jack A.; F/L, 630 Squadron, RAFVR.
Watson, A.; Sapper, Royal Engineers 1939-41, RASC 1941-46.
Watson, David; Major, 22nd Cheshire Regiment.
Watson, John Liversidge; 1634473 Gunner, Royal Artillery.
Weaver, J.W.; W/Bombadier, Royal Artillery.
Wheatley, G.; Lieutenant, Royal Sussex Regiment.
Wheeler, Dr. K.M.; RAMC 1941-46.
Whelan, John Aloysius; Cpl, Gordon Highlanders.
Whiteland, A.A.J.; LAC, RAF.
Whittle, B.J.; Blue Funnel Line, Liverpool.
Wilkinson, P.J.; L/Sgt, 1st, 2nd, 3rd Battalions Grenadier Guards.
Williams, D.; 844441 Sgt, Royal Regiment of Artillery 1939-45
Williams, Eileen.
Wimhurst, John C.; RAF, RBL Norbury Branch President.
Withers, Brian; Guardsman, Grenadier Guards.
Wright, Mrs Bertha (née Jones); 2141431 Aircraft Mechanic, 1942-46.
Wyres, William Joseph; 607648 Pte, Queen's Royal Regiment, 1914-19.

Y

Young, H.V.; Technician, Royal Corps of Signals. Africa Star, 1939-45 Star, Italy Star, France-Germany Star, Victoria Medal, GS Medal.
Young, W.E.; Cpl, Royal Ulster Rifles 1949-65; Sgt Royal Corps of Transport 1966-90.

Z

Zahra, Vincent P.; Bombadier, 8th S/L Battery, Royal Malta Artillery. 1939-45 Star, 1939-45 War Medal, Africa Star.

In Memoriam

Baines, John W.; Captain, ! Div., RASC. MBE.

Bracey, George Ernest; 5191635, Pte, 10th Battalion, Gloucestershire Regiment. Died in Burma 1.1.95.

Greenwood, Charles E.; Captain, 8th Battalion, Parachute Regiment.

Grigg, C.F.; Cpl, RAF.

Groom, H.D.T.; Captain, Royal West Kent Regiment, Royal Army Pay Corps.

Handley, T.G.; 2360675 Pte, Royal Corps of Signals. POW, taken at Dunkirk, 1940, returned home 6th June 1945.

Hearne, J.A.; RAOC 1943-46. 'Memories of a dear brother.'

Hearne, Peter; 7366078 Pte, RAMC, 6th Airborne Division. Died on Sword Beach 6th June 1944, aged 25. 'In loving memory of my father - memories of you I will always keep.'

Hill, Arthur; Major, Lincolnshire Regiment. Killed at Koima Ridge, Burma.

Hill, Harry George; Quartermaster Sgt, Royal Horse Artillery.

Hill, H.Walter; Captain, Royal Signals.

Lambon, Alfred Edward, 5110510; Private, Royal Warwickshire Regiment and Glider Pilot Regiment.

Mole, A.G.T.; Captain, 1st Division, RASC

Mole, G.P.; Captain, Intelligence Corps.

Standing, Derick; Lieutenant. AAC pilot killed flying casualty evacuation flight in Canada, aged 22 years.

Tyrrell, Edward; Pte, 2nd Battalion, Parachute Regiment.